Lucy Letby is Guilty?

Luke Armitage

Other Books by Luke Armitage

Mary Bell - The Real Story

Contents

INTRODUCTION

Lucy Letby is guilty. That's the starting point of any discussion about this case. She was found guilty and is now in prison. Barring a minor miracle she is going to be prison for a very long time. Probably forever. But a number of people do not believe Lucy Letby is guilty. They do not believe she is an evil serial killer nurse. They think she is innocent and this has all been an almighty screw-up by the health system, doctors, the police, and the courts. And then you've got a number of people who have no idea if Lucy Letby is guilty or innocent but are not convinced the prosecution evidence at the trial was strong enough for a conviction. The final group in this true crime culture war (if we can use that term) are the people who are certain Lucy Letby is guilty and baffled by all these people online defending a baby killer and acting as if she's a lovely sweet woman who has been the victim of the greatest miscarriage in history since the last greatest miscarriage in history. All of these people can't be right can they? At least one of these groups must be barking up the wrong tree.

Writing a book about Lucy Letby is a bit of a fool's errand as this story seems to be constantly evolving. At the time of writing the Thirwall Inquiry is still ongoing and who knows what might happen in the future. Maybe one day Letby's barrister will pull a rabbit out of a hat and win an appeal. Or perhaps more damning evidence of guilt will surface. The problem with writing a book about the Letby case at the moment is that your book is inevitably out of date as soon as it is finished. So what I've tried to do in this book is cover what has happened since the trial and make it as up to date as possible. If you are interested in the Letby case and have been following this story you are probably familiar by now with Letby's early life and what happened at the trial so I have eschewed most of that stuff to focus on the right to appeal bid, the Child K retrial, and the Thirwall Inquiry.

A big theme of this book too is the schism of opinion which opened up online. You have forums and groups which believe Letby is guilty and forums and groups which think Letby is innocent. People often seem to retreat to their own little echo chamber when it comes to the Letby case. Now you might think that groups of people online talking about and debating the Letby case and having different opinions is no big deal and you'd probably be right about that. The debate has taken on a new dimension now though with some medical professionals openly questioning the conclusions which were drawn by the prosecution in the conviction of Lucy Letby. This is really the main hope for Lucy Letby and anyone who represents her in the future. They'll need some heavyweight medical opinion in their corner to have any hope of making the authorities look at her case again.

It doesn't really matter what people on online forums say about the case and it doesn't matter what journalists write about the case. It probably doesn't matter what statisticians say about the case either. But it does matter if respected medical professionals openly start to question the convictions because these figures carry the most weight in a complex medical themed crime case debate like the Letby affair. This does though add yet another layer of complexity to the case because it creates a situation where you have experts disagreeing with experts. As of yet it is hard to say if there will ever be enough contrary medical opinion to shift any dials when it comes to the Letby case. There isn't at the moment but you can easily find dissenting opinions among doctors.

A salient difference between the sceptical medical

professionals and more general online supporters of Letby is that the medical professionals will tend to say they have no idea if Letby is guilty or innocent but have concerns about the evidence which was used to convict her. Your more general online Lucy Letby supporter often tends to be 100% convinced that she is innocent. The statisticians who have taken an interest in this case also seem to lean towards Letby being innocent. Statisticians never seem to think anyone is guilty do they? We'll talk about that in this book and test whether or not that is true. It should be noted that the weight of medical opinion is still against Lucy Letby. The medical experts and doctors who gave evidence at the trial have not changed their mind.

The Thirwall Inquiry has also not been a great boost to any claims of Letby being innocent. Authors of hospital reports which some claimed exonerated Letby have said at Thirwall that wasn't the case at all and there have also been new details of suspicious and odd behaviour by Letby in the past (failing her first nursing placement, giving unprescribed drugs to infants, giving a baby too much morphine, allegedly dislodging breathing tubes in Liverpool etc). Of course, Letby supporters will say that Thirwall is a whitewash and biased and one-sided. That's the way this debate goes. It becomes a giant looping circle. In this book we will try to look at both sides of the debate while also respecting the current status of the case. Later on, a chapter will set out the reasons why Letby might be innocent and then the following chapter will set out the reasons why she was found guilty. This book is not explicitly designed to change anyone's mind about the case or challenge the prosecution but it will acknowledge that not everyone agrees with the trial verdict and seek to understand why some people have very grave doubts about the safety of the convictions.

THE RETRIAL

Lucy Letby is a former neonatal nurse convicted of murdering seven infants and attempting the murder of seven others between June 2015 and June 2016. Letby was working at the Countess of Chester Hospital at the time. The general facts of this case and the convictions will be broadly familiar to the reader by now. The trial was one of the longest in English legal history. When the verdict was rendered it wasn't uncommon for Letby to be compared to Myra Hindley in the media. But the conviction wasn't the end of the story. It was only the beginning. There remained an unquantifiable number of people online who disagreed with the conviction and insisted that Lucy Letby was innocent. This unexpected movement only seems to have become louder as the months and years rolled on. This is something which those involved in prosecuting the trial have found surprising and even frustrating. One can only imagine how the parents of the infants who died must feel to have to listen to this debate. How do they get closure on this terrible case when people keep insisting that Lucy Letby is innocent and the trial was a gross miscarriage of justice? Do these claims have any validity?

Miscarriages of justice have happened and do happen. There will be more in the future because a legal system is not infallible. We can all probably dredge up some famous examples where an innocent person was wrongly convicted for a terrible crime. Take the Jill Dando murder case for example. The police were convinced that a local oddball named Barry George, who lived a few streets away from Jill Dando's home in Fulham, was the killer. George was arrested and convicted but the highly dubious gunshot residue evidence used to convict him was later deemed unsafe. A tiny minuscule+ speck of firearms reside was found in one of

George's coat pockets. However, George (who was very eccentric) would sometimes leave fireworks in his coat pockets and there was also the possibility of contamination (the coat was photographed at the police station near where firearms were photographed). Last but not least was the fact that the police never found any evidence that Barry George even owned a gun in the first place. The gun used to kill Jill Dando was highly unusual and modified. This meant that Barry George was either a gun craftsman or had underworld criminal connections. Neither of these scenarios seemed very plausible.

Despite the insistence of the police with their stalker theory there was never any compelling evidence that Barry George had any particular interest in Jill Dando. The house in Fulham where Dando was killed was one she didn't even live in anymore and was in the process of selling. She had moved house and only gone back there briefly to check for mail. How did Barry George know she would be there at this precise moment? Barry George didn't drive and was an overweight man with famously bad co-ordination and low intelligence so how did he manage to escape from the murder scene so swiftly without attracting any incriminating eyewitnesses? One can see then, in this particular example, the conviction of Barry George was always highly questionable and full of seemingly implausible details. There simply did not appear to be sufficient evidence to conclude with any degree of certainty that Barry George killed Jill Dando. It came as no great surprise that he was eventually released after a successful appeal.

Many might also remember the shameful case of Stefan Kiszko. Stefan Kiszko was a man with learning difficulties who was convicted for the murder of eleven year-old Lesley Molseed in 1975. Kiszko turned out to be completely innocent and was later released - though not before he had spent sixteen harrowing years in prison for a crime he didn't commit. In July 1992, Rachel Nickell was murdered on Wimbledon Common. Rachel was with her two-year old son at the time and stabbed nearly fifty times. Her throat was slit and she was sexually assaulted. It was a horrendous attack. A man named Colin Stagg was arrested for the murder. The police had zeroed in on Colin Stagg as a suspect because he walked his dog on Wimbledon Common and fitted an offender profile they had composed in relation to the killer. They even set up a 'honey trap' for Stagg in which a female police officer posed as a woman who was romantically interested in him. The objective of the female police officer was to gain the confidence of Stagg and see if he confessed to the murder. Colin Stagg never did confess though because he was innocent. It was in fact a lunatic named Robert Napper who had murdered Rachel Nickell.

In the 1990s, two women named Sally Clark and Donna Anthony were convicted of murdering their young children. The women were innocent and later acquitted - though not before their lives had been ruined. Clark was convicted on the basis of flawed statistical evidence presented by paediatrician Dr Roy Meadow. When it comes to the medical world and mistakes there was the fairly recent case of the unexplained deaths of several patients at Stepping Hill Hospital. Low blood sugar levels were discovered in some patients - leading to a theory that saline solution had been contaminated with insulin. A young nurse named Rebecca Leighton was arrested on suspicion of foul play and placed in prison as a case against her was prepared. It turned out that the main evidence against Deighton was a thumbprint from her had been found on a saline bag which appeared to have been damaged by a needle. The problem with this evidence though was that other members of staff had touched this bag too. The authorities soon realised the evidence against Rebecca Leighton was exceptionally weak to the point of being invisible so she was cleared and released after spending a month and a half in prison.

One of the hospital deaths deemed to be suspicious at Stepping Hill had occurred after Rebecca Leighton was no longer working there. It was patently ludicrous that she had become a suspect. Rebecca Leighton, despite clearing her name, was later found to have stolen medicines from the hospital and so struggled to get work in the health service afterwards. A male nurse named Victorino Chua was eventually convicted for the deaths at Stepping Hill. Chua was convicted of injecting saline drips and ampoules with insulin. It later came to light that Chua, a Filipino national, may have faked the qualifications he used to get into Britain to take up a nursing position. In parallel with the Lucy Letby case, the police found notes in Chua's house in which he called himself 'evil' and appeared to be confessing to something. The importance of the infamous post-it-notes in the Letby case were certainly one of the more contestable facets. They were written on the advice of a counsellor and not taken seriously by criminologists who study this type of thing. Another thing Victorino Chua had in common with Lucy Letby is that no motive was ever established.

The prosecutor in the Stepping Hill case later described it as being like 'Murder on the Orient Express with 700 suspects on the train'. Getting to the bottom of alleged unexplained deaths in a hospital is, for all manner of obvious reasons, considerably more complicated than investigating deaths elsewhere. The trial of Lucy Letby was not one in which anyone would have wanted to be called for jury service. Not only was the case upsetting but it involved highly complex and detailed medical evidence. There is an argument that cases like this should be decided by an expert medical panel rather than a jury. The thing is though that doctors and professors sometimes disagree with one another too.

The complexity of alleged medical murders cases and the lack of unanimity in the medical field is highlighted by the strange case of Dr John Bodkin Adams. Adams was born in 1899 in Randalstown, Country Antrim. Whether or not he was serial killer is still open to question. He was suspected of murdering over a hundred of his patients for financial gain but was acquitted of the one charge of murder he did face.

It could be that Adams was simply an advocate of assisted dying. It could also be though that he was the forerunner to Harold Shipman. The real truth was never really established. Adams was a doctor in the town of Eastbourne and had many elderly patients. It transpired that around 132 of these patients changed their will to include Adams before they died. That seems more than a little suspicious doesn't it? Why would anyone change their will near the end of their life and leave money and valuables to their doctor? Wouldn't you want the money to go to your relatives instead? John Bodkin Adams attracted suspicion in Eastbourne because two of his deceased patients even left him a Rolls-Royce in their will. There were certainly alarms about Adams. One family complained that their relative got worse because Adams kept injecting her with morphine. There were also accounts of how he was the wealthiest doctor in England and living a lavish lifestyle. Where was he getting all this money from?

Adams was even accused of killing one patient with an overdose of sleeping pills. He was naturally named in the will of this patient once they had expired. When a woman named Amy Ware died in his care, Adams said he was not a beneficiary in her will EVEN though he was. Why did he lie about this? Annabelle Kilgour died in 1950 after Adams gave her extra strong sedatives. In her will she left him £200 and a clock. Julia Bradnum, a patient of Adams, died in 1952 at the age of 85. Adams persuaded Bradnum to sell her house before she died and she left him £600 in her will. Hilda Neil Miller, who was 85, died in 1952 while being treated by Adams. A relative of Hilda said she saw Adams rifling through Hilda's valuables and pocketing things after she died. Adams then quickly arranged the burial himself. There were countless suspicious incidents like this relating to Dr John Bodkin Adams. The whispers and gossip surrounding Dr Adams got so intense that the police began investigating the wills of his patients and arrested him. They focused in particular on the death of Edith Alice Morrell.

Morrell was a patient of Dr Adams who died from a cocktail of heroin and morphine given to her by the doctor. Adams was left some money and a Rolls Royce as a result of her death. Dr John Bodkin Adams, thanks to a rather shrewd QC, was cleared of charges of murder. What saved him was that the nurses looking after Morrell had been forced to concede they kept detailed notes on her treatment. The nurses suspected Adams of foul play but nothing in their notes proved it. The prosecution also failed to find any fellow doctors willing to argue that this was a clear case of murder. One strange thing that also went in favour of Dr John Bodkin Adams was the fact that he also managed to avoid having to give any evidence himself. He wasn't questioned in court. After the trial, Adams was struck off the medical register for forging prescriptions. Amazingly though he was reinstated as a GP in 1961. Would you want to be treated by a doctor suspected of killing over a hundred of his patients? Adams later became President (and Honorary Medical Officer) of the British Clay Pigeon Shooting Association. He died in 1983.

Though friends believed he was innocent much of the media and public always thought Adams was guilty. Dr Adams, at his trial, had the flip reverse of Lucy Letby in court. They couldn't find a doctor willing to testify on behalf of the prosecution when Adams was on trial. During the trial of Lucy Letby, not a single medical expert was called by the defence. Lucy Letby's defence team called only one person to the witness box. The defence witness was a plumber who worked at the hospital in Chester. The plumber spoke about how the sinks sometimes got blocked. He said the plumbing and hygiene in this NHS hospital could have been better. There probably isn't an NHS hospital in the country where one couldn't make this observation. By the time the trial was over everyone (apart it seems from John Sweeney and some of Letby's online advocates) had forgotten about the plumber and his evidence. But people did wonder why the defence team chose not to call any medical experts to give evidence. To some observers this was such a strange decision that it called into question the fairness of Letby's trial. The basic argument of these observers was that the jury only got to hear one side of the story.

A large number of doctors, professors, and medical experts gave evidence during the trial but none of them were called by the defence. That is to say, none of them cast serious doubt on the safety of convicting Lucy Letby based on the available medical evidence. Ben Myers KC was in charge of Letby's defence at the trial. The jury were plainly not going to acquit Lucy Letby on account of a few blocked sinks. They needed alternative takes from medical professionals - not tales of sewage. So why did Myers only call a plumber as a witness? Ben Myers is obviously not stupid. He must have judged that calling a medical expert to the witness box might not be in the best interests of Lucy Letby. Ben Myers had access to much more information than anyone currently debating Lucy Letby online. If he decided that calling a medical witness might undermine Lucy Letby we must ask why this was the case. A witness called in an English trial has a duty to the court and not the side who have called the witness or instructed them. This meant that if a doctor or medical expert was called by the defence they would not be specifically there to exonerate Lucy Letby. They would simply be there to answer medical questions in relation to the case to the best of their ability with complete honesty.

Mr Myers had no guarantee then that such evidence would always land in Lucy Letby's favour. The prosecution at Letby's trial was led by Nick Johnson KC. Johnson was a skilled and effective cross-examiner and Myers probably wasn't wildly enthusiastic about Johnson having too many witnesses put up by the defence to question. The core strategy of Ben Myers in court was twofold. He highlighted what the defence saw as care failings in the hospital and also argued that the infants in the unit where Lucy Letby worked where not nearly as 'robust' and healthy as the prosecution suggested. The defence believed that when these two factors were combined the 'cluster' of infant deaths which attracted suspicion was thus explained. In their view then, Lucy Letby was made a scapegoat for care failings. A key strategy of Ben Myers in court was also to attack the credibility of Dr Dewi Evans, the chief prosecution witness. Dr Evans has since become the main panto villain for online defenders of Lucy Letby. It was Dewi Evans who reviewed all the cases at the hospital for the police and decided there were some clear instances of deliberate harm. Dr Evans attributed a number of deaths to the injection of air (air embolism). Other experts who gave evidence at the trial broadly seemed to agree with this theory. But some medical professionals have their doubts about the air embolism diagnosis.

One theory as to why no medical witnesses were called by the defence is that Ben Myers was confident that he could isolate Dr Evans as a weak (and most important) link in the prosecution and put him under pressure in court. Myers may have judged that this would be sufficient (or at least the best strategy) and calling in other experts might unbalance the case for the defence because these experts might well have points of agreement with the prosecution. Myers hammered away at Dr Evans in court, which led to a few testy exchanges, but a barrister debating medical evidence with a doctor is never going to win a clear cut victory. Ben Myers argued the case against Lucy Letby was circumstantial - which is an opinion that many others share. A lot of convictions are circumstantial though. There isn't always a smoking gun. A jury has to decide, based on the evidence, what they THINK was most likely to have happened. Sometimes this is relatively straight forward and at other times, as with Lucy Letby, this is complex and requires months of evidence (and even after all of this some people still disagree on the verdict).

Dr Michael Hall is a retired neonatologist who was available for the defence in preparation for the Letby trial. The defence will almost certainly have formed parts of their strategy around what they learned from Dr Hall. However, for some reason, Dr Hall was not called to give evidence at the trial. His subsequent media comments suggest he was frustrated by this decision and would like to have spoken at Lucy Letby's trial. Dr Hall believed that the infants at the hospital were not as stable as the prosecution made out and he also felt the evidence presented in relation to the victims being injected with air was weak and questionable. So why was he not asked to give evidence at the trial? According to Dr Hall it was Lucy Letby who didn't want him to give evidence. It seems unlikely that she made this decision independently. Letby would almost certainly have been following the advice of her barrister Ben Myers. It seems logical to presume that Ben

Myers did not much relish the prospect of Dr Hall being cross-examined by Nick Johnson KC. Myers may have judged that the defence case was sufficient as it was and might be weakened by presenting the jury with yet more complex evidence. There was also the rather obvious fact that a great number of doctors and experts had given evidence at the trial. How credible would one lone doctor potentially be going against this general consensus?

The Dutch nurse Lucia de Berk worked at the Juliana Kinderziekenhuis, a children's hospital in The Hague. Between 2000 and 2001 there were nine cases of infant death or collapse at the hospital. Lucia de Berk was judged to be the common denominator. Charges were filed and a medical expert testified that the first 'victim' had been administered digoxin. Digoxin is a medication used to treat various heart conditions, primarily to manage heart failure and atrial fibrillation (an irregular and often rapid heart rate). Lucia de Berk was found guilty. She was now officially a medical serial killer. She got life in prison for the murders of four patients and the attempted murders of three others. Throughout this, Lucia de Berk always maintained her innocence - which was not exactly unusual as most criminals (especially killers) pretend they are innocent. In the case of Lucia de Berk she wasn't pretending though. She genuinely was innocent of the charges. A number of journalists and scientists came forward to support Lucia de Berk. In the end the case was re-opened. It turned out that the statistical evidence which had played a role in convicting her was wrong. The expert medical opinion that the first victim had been administered digoxin was also wrong.

Further investigation found that the infant deaths at the Juliana Kinderziekenhuis were natural and not as a result of foul play. Lucia de Berk was cleared and released in 2010. Her nightmare lasted for over six years before she was exonerated. Lucia de Berk is a name that often crops up in relation to the Lucy Letby case. A plank in the prosecution of Lucia de Berk was that she had written a form of confession notes. We saw something similar in the Letby case. Lucia de Berk's notes were apparently simply fiction for a book she was writing. As for Letby's notes, they were apparently suggested by a therapist as a way to let off steam. It is probably natural to wonder if Lucy Letby might possibly be another Lucia de Berk. Letby's most fervent supporters don't just wonder. They are already convinced that we have something akin to Lucia de Berk II: The Sequel in the Letby case. Some of them believe the two cases will end in the same way. Letby's convictions will be quashed and she'll walk free from prison. The odds of this happening don't appear to be very short though at this specific time of writing.

One potential problem is that not every single hospital/medical themed murder case can be another Lucia de Berk. Some of them have to be real don't they? Medical serial killers are not fictitious cryptids. There have actually been a fair few of them in real life. 36% of serial killers in England this century were nurses. Where does it end if every murder/foul play case in a hospital or involving a doctor or nurse is treated with scepticism and disdain and dismissed as sub-optimal care or a cover-up? What about Beverly Allitt? Was she innocent? Should that case be re-opened? This might sound like sarcasm on my part but at least one supporter of Lucy Letby has suggested aloud that Beverly Allit was probably innocent too. If we refuse to believe that medical serial killers actually exist then we are going to make life much easier for the next one to come along. By the same token though a very high bar must be set when it comes to the burden of proof in such cases. This is the catalyst for the division of opinion which has steadily grown since Letby's trial. To put it in simple terms; a number of people don't believe the case against Letby was strong enough to say with absolute certainty she was guilty. In their opinion the high burden of proof required for such horrific convictions was not met.

Lucy Letby's options are fairly limited. She could go to the Criminal Cases Review Commission but they would have to review the case afresh (which would take a very long time) and then it would be put back to the Court of Appeal - who would most likely reject the appeal again. The Court of Appeal is not going to re-open the case unless new evidence is presented which conclusively proves that Letby didn't harm those infants. This evidence, should it exist, is going to be medical rather than statistical. At the trial, Letby's defence team didn't really bother too much with statistical evidence and neither did the prosecution. The main focus of the defence was their claim that the infants were not stable and the hospital was failing. After the statistical blunder was exposed, the case against Lucia de Berk completely fell apart when the digoxin diagnosis was proven to be questionable and mistaken. This led to a review of the case - the conclusion of which judged that the infant deaths were not a result of intentional harm. Letby would need something along these lines in order to quash her convictions or have the case reviewed.

Lucy Letby ended up at HMP Bronzefield in Surrey. Previous prisoners at Bronzefield have included Rosemary West, Karen Matthews, and Joanna Dennehy. The most notorious current inmate of the prison is Sharon Carr. In 1992, Sharon Carr gruesomely murdered a hairdresser named Katie Rackliff by stabbing her over thirty times. Carr was just twelve years-old at the time. Two years later, the now fourteen year-old Carr stabbed a fellow pupil (who mercifully survived) in the toilets at her comprehensive school. There was no motive for the attacks. Carr was just a dangerous and disturbed psychopath who enjoyed stabbing people. Sharon Carr was locked up for the school attack but it was only while she was incarcerated that the authorities realised she had murdered Katie Rackliff. This was the type of company Lucy Letby was keeping these days. Salsa loving Lucy was as infamous as any of them when it came down down to the stark reality of charge sheets. It was head scratching that a young dedicated nurse had somehow ended up in this ghoulish company.

A neonatal unit, where Letby worked, commonly referred to as a neonatal intensive care unit (NICU), is a special medical facility designed to provide intensive care for new born infants, particularly those born prematurely or with medical conditions that require immediate attention. The structure and function of a neonatal unit are crucial in ensuring the well-being and survival of these vulnerable new-borns. Neonatal units are typically located within hospitals and are equipped with specialised medical equipment to support the needs of critically ill new-borns. The physical layout of a neonatal unit is designed to provide a controlled and sterile environment, with individual rooms or bays for each infant to minimise the risk of infections. Neonatal units are equipped with state-of-the-art medical equipment, including incubators, ventilators, monitors, and infusion pumps. These devices are essential for monitoring and supporting the new-born's vital functions, providing oxygen therapy, and administering medications.

Neonatal units are staffed by a team of highly trained healthcare professionals, including neonatologists, neonatal nurses, respiratory therapists, and other specialists. The neonatal team works collaboratively to provide 24/7 care for the infants, ensuring that they receive the appropriate medical treatment and support. The primary function of a neonatal unit is to provide medical care for new born infants who require specialised treatment. This may include monitoring vital signs, administering medications, providing respiratory support, and managing medical conditions such as jaundice, infections, and respiratory distress syndrome. One of the primary duties of a neonatal nurse is to provide direct patient care to new born infants. This includes monitoring vital signs, administering medications, and performing procedures such as feeding tube insertions and IV placements. Neonatal nurses must be skilled in assessing the condition of their patients and responding swiftly to any changes in their health status.

In June, 2024, Lucy Letby was back in court for a retrial over the death of the child known as Child K. In the original trial the jury could not reach a verdict on Child K. Lucy Letby was now 34 years-old and looked very different (and a lot wearier) now with her natural light brown hair (she wasn't really a blonde). The retrial took place at Manchester Crown Court. Although there were some criticisms (from Letby supporters) of Letby's defence team and Ben Myers KC after the trial (the most obvious criticism was their decision not to call any medical or statistical experts as witnesses), Letby seemed to have faith in Myers. He led the defence at the Child K retrial. Nick Johnson KC, who was in the prosecution corner, said at the retrial that 'Apgar' scores for Child K were ranked at 9/10 ten minutes after birth. This is above average and indicates a perfectly stable baby. Child K was the case where Dr Ravi Jayaram was the on-call consultant. Dr Jayaram said that when the baby crashed he found Letby in there with the infant doing nothing to help. By now he (and other consultants) had suspicions about Letby and Jayaram said it was a sort of instinct which made him go in the room.

The machines connected to Child K should have sounded an alarm if there was a problem but they did not. Nick Johnson told the retrial that Letby had disabled the alarm. Not just that but she had been caught 'red handed' by Dr Jayaram. Lucy Letby was not assigned to Child K but 'made it her business' to attend to this baby. This was the general tenor of the evidence presented by Nick Johnson. The prosecution detailed how the breathing tube for Child K was dislodged more than once and suggested this was not a random coincidence. Anyone who covered the original trial would have felt a pang of deja vu as Nick Johnson and Ben Myers resumed their duties for the prosecution and defence respectively and a panoply of complex medical jargon back and forth commenced. Ben Myers told the jury the previous trial had no relevance to this specific case (Child K). They had to focus only on the evidence presented to them in the days to come. Myers had actually complained about this retrial because he argued it was impossible for Letby to get a fair hearing given the inevitable amount of bad publicity surrounding her in the media after the original trial. It was obviously nigh on impossible to find a jury who were not aware of Letby and what she had been convicted of doing.

Mr Myers, for the defence, said there was no hospital record of where Dr Jayaram was or what he was doing when Child K desaturated. It was simply his word, or memory, that we were being asked to believe. Ben Myers pointed out that Child K was born premature and should have been in a more specialist unit (a transfer was being arranged for the infant but this could only be done once it was deemed stable enough for the journey). A few days later, Dr Jayaram entered the witness box to give evidence. Dr Jayaram was an interesting figure in the Lucy Letby case because supporters of Letby's innocence will often say there was no evidence of her being caught in the act of doing anything wrong. Dr Jayaram was the counter to this - sort of but not quite. Therein lies the rub with this case when it comes to opposing views on Letby's conviction. Everything is debated and nothing can be accepted. Dr Jayaram said that by the time of Child K's collapse there were already concerns about Lucy Letby among a small group of doctors. They had begun to speculate among themselves if she was to blame for the rash of deaths and collapses that seemed to plague the neonatal unit.

Dr Jayaram said he decided to go and check on Lucy Letby to set his mind at rest and then found her standing there as the baby desaturated. In medical terminology, desaturation refers to a decrease in the saturation of oxygen in the blood, typically measured as a percentage of hemoglobin molecules carrying oxygen. Desaturation can indicate a variety of clinical conditions, such as respiratory distress, pulmonary issues, or problems with the cardiovascular system. It is an important parameter in monitoring patients. Dr Jayaram said he asked Lucy Letby what she was doing and Letby replied that the baby was desaturating. Dr Jayaram then attended to the baby (and was assisted by Dr Smith). Dr Jayaram said at the Child K retrial that it was 'beyond coincidence' for him to find Lucy Letby standing over a desaturating baby with the alarms mysteriously not working. Ben Myers KC had established through questioning another member of staff that it was not unusual for nurses to check on rooms and babies to which they were they not officially assigned. This, so the prosecution hoped, dented the perception of Letby roaming around of her own accord to isolate a victim. The defence argued that Letby's movements were perfectly normal for a nurse and should not be construed as suspicious or out of the ordinary.

Ben Myers asked Dr Jayaram more than once if he had 'got' Letby or caught her 'red handed' by walking in on her with

Child K. Was this proof, seen with his own eyes, that Lucy Letby was a hospital serial killer? Dr Jayaram could not quite answer this question directly and for good reason. He had not mentioned the incident in his medical notes for the day and had said nothing to his bosses about Letby allegedly dislodging a tube. He did not call the police or report this incident to the hospital management. He did not even discuss the matter with Lucy Letby. Ben Myers asked Dr Jayaram why this was the case. If he suspected Letby of harming infants why did he not record this in his medical notes? Why did he not call the police or report the incident to the hospital bosses? Dr Jayaram said he regretted not 'escalating' the matter at the time. He explained that his immediate preoccupation was Child K. He decided not to report the incident to the management because he feared they would brush the matter under the carpet. He did not call the police because he felt he needed more time to discuss this matter with other doctors.

Dr Jayaram said cognitive dissonance was at play and he didn't want to believe his fears about Letby. Jayaram told the retrial he couldn't run around the hospital telling everyone that Letby might be a serial killer. It needed a more thoughtful and collaborative approach. "We spent a long time trying to raise concerns... and running into walls. Had I had more courage, maybe I would've picked up the phone and called police." Ben Myers KC pointed out that in his original police interview Dr Jayaram said he couldn't remember if an alarm sounded when Child K desaturated with Letby in the room but now - in the retrial of Baby K - he was sure there was no alarm. This was a discrepancy. Dr Jayaram answered this by saying it was not an alarm which made him go into the room. His motivation was his nagging suspicion that he needed to check on Letby. The point Ben Myers was making in court was that, in the view of the defence, Dr Jayaram had a bias against Lucy Letby. This meant that he saw everything Letby did as suspicious - even when she was doing nothing wrong. Dr Jayaram's response to this was to say that at the time he trusted the 'system' and the hospital but now realised that had been the wrong approach.

Regarding the alarm for the baby monitor equipment, the alarm is supposed to go off if any adverse readings are recorded for the baby. The electronics engineer for the hospital supplied a statement for the retrial in which he explained that the alarm could be turned off by a member of staff. There was a pause button and also a silence function. The implication of the prosecution was that Lucy Letby used one of these functions to pause the alarm. However, there were other nurses who recalled hearing an alarm. One can see then how confusing a medical themed trial can be. Literally every scrap of evidence was subject to conflicting tangents. Establishing a precise timeline was very complex. One of the things Letby was accused of was dislodging intubation tubes on purpose. An intubation tube is a medical device used to secure an airway in patients who are unable to breathe adequately on their own. This tube is inserted through the mouth or nose and is typically connected to a ventilator or anesthesia machine, allowing for mechanical ventilation. Another nurse at the retrial said it was unusual for a baby as small as Child K to dislodge its own own tube. Unusual but not impossible.

Lucy Letby was put in the witness box at the retrial for the Child K case. This was seen as surprising because the defence case in the original trial was certainly dented when Letby gave evidence. Letby came across as controlled and unemotional which, whether fair or not, saw her portrayed in court sketches as a cold and aloof sort of person. Lucy Letby answered a lot of questions by saying she 'couldn't remember' in the original trial. While it is true that recall of medical details/movements on specific dates years prior would be a challenge for anyone (most of us would probably struggle to remember what we had for dinner the day before yesterday) the foggy memory of Lucy Letby was not much help to her case. The biggest problem that Letby ran into at the Child K retrial was coming up with a convincing rebuttal when Nick Johnson KC pressed her on the incident where Dr Jayaram said he found her standing over the desaturating baby apparently doing nothing to help. The implication of the prosecution was that Letby had caused the problem in the first place and then paused the alarm - whereupon she was 'caught' by Dr Jayaram.

At the retrial, Letby disputed Dr Jayaram's version of events and said this did not happen. She didn't recall that incident where he walked in on her. It didn't happen. The problem for Letby was that in three rounds of police interviews before the original trial she had not disputed this incident and accepted that it probably happened. By way of explanation, Letby said to the police that she may have been waiting a moment for the baby to correct itself before taking action. Now, in court, Letby was denying that this incident happened at all. The prosecution saw this as a strong piece of evidence for them because it suggested that Letby had accepted this in police interviews because she presumed they must have hospital evidence which would make any denial pointless. In her police interviews, Letby did not deny the incident happened but instead placed her focus on her own explanation to what she was doing. By the time of the trials, Letby realised they had no hard evidence for the incident happening and it was merely her word against the word of Dr Jayaram. This is why (so the prosecution theory went) she had shifted her position and no longer acknowledged that the incident occurred. Letby did not like Dr Jayaram because he was one of the doctors who sparked the theory that she might be harming infants.

Lucy Letby probably had her fill of Nick Johnson in the first trial but she was having to face him again now. Letby seemed slightly more confident and less meek than in the first trial but her memory didn't seem to be much better than it was the first time around. Letby commented to Mr Johnson at one point that he was going round in circles. Little flashes of defiance like this were largely absent from the first trial. Letby insisted that giving an infant a moment to correct itself was policy at the Countess of Chester Hospital. Letby told Mr Johnson that at her police interviews she 'assumed' that Dr Jayaram must have been right because she couldn't remember much about Child K and was vague on details. She disputed his version of events now because having thought about it she now realised there was no incident as Dr Jayaram described of her acting suspiciously as the baby crashed.

Mr Johnson disputed Letby's claim that she couldn't remember much about Child K and said Letby had done an online search related to the deceased infant and its family ten weeks before she was interviewed for the police. One inference drawn from Johnson's comment is that Letby was aware the police would get involved sooner or later and was 'prepping' to get her story straight. Letby said she had no memory of this online search and couldn't say why she had done it. One fact which came to light for the retrial was that the swipe card data from the hospital used in Lucy Letby's original trial was wrong. The neonatal unit, for obvious security reasons (you don't want anyone just waltzing in), required a staff security card to be swiped before you could enter. It was revealed that the police had misread this data and interpreted the data as people leaving the unit when in fact it was people arriving. In essence then, the police had got the swipe card data back to front. Some of those who either believe Letby is innocent or remain unconvinced by her guilt saw this as something which had the potential to be very significant indeed.

That view however did not seem to be shared by Ben Myers KC. He agreed with Nick Johnson that it was an honest mistake and did not make a fuss about it. We can only conclude then that in the view of Mr Myers the swipe card mistake did not make any notable difference to the case. If the swipe data had been a potential lifeline to Letby and important to the case then you can be certain that Mr Myers would have kicked up a big fuss about it. Swipe card data can be unreliable as evidence because people sometimes use their card and hold the door open for others. The data can never be entirely accurate. To the surprise of just about no one, not even her most optimistic supporters, Lucy Letby was found guilty in the Child K retrial and sentenced to a 15th whole life term. Having another life sentence added to her slate didn't really make much difference to Letby at this point. She was either going to die in prison or some Lucia de Berk style twist was going to happen one day and Letby's convictions would be quashed. A 15th sentence didn't alter that. The 15th sentence was though vitally important to the parents and relatives of Child K. At least they had some grain of closure and a sense that justice was done. Those who remained agnostic about Letby's guilt/innocence and those who believed she was innocent did not have their minds changed by the Child K trial. "I'm innocent," said Letby as she was led away in court.

THE APPEAL

Dr John Bodkin Adams was shrewd not to give evidence at his trial. Lucy Letby did speak at her main trial but her performance was not tremendously helpful to the defence. It was cited by some observers as a key turning point in the trial. Letby's cross-examination by Nick Johnson at her 2023 trial did not go very well. She came across as bored, nonchalant, indifferent, and aloof in court. She did not display any of the anger or defiance you would expect of someone who claimed to be innocent and showed no emotion at any of the shattering evidence in relation to infant deaths. The only times Letby showed emotion was when the doctor she apparently had a crush on gave evidence and when a photograph of her bedroom was shown. Letby also damaged her own defence by agreeing with the prosecution on salient points - like insulin poisoning. She did of course insist that she wasn't responsible but did agree it appeared to have happened. Ben Myers probably couldn't win whatever he did. If there had been a no show from Letby when it came to giving evidence that might have looked bad to the jury. Putting her in the witness box was also laced with risk - as turned out to be the case.

If, as the prosecution alleged, there was foul play at work in the hospital in relation to the spike in deaths, the perpetrator of these crimes could only be Lucy Letby. Lucy Letby was the one who others at the hospital pointed the finger of suspicion at. She was the one who exhibited odd behaviour according to parents. She was the nurse on shift the most times when these things happened. She was the one who took home handover sheets and even a paper towel from a waste paper bin which had resuscitation notes in relation to one of the deaths. None of these facts were absolute proof of guilt but if the serial killer theory was applied, and in this case it was obviously was applied, then Lucy Letby was the most logical culprit. This wasn't like the Rebecca Leighton case where there turned out to be another much more plausible suspect.

In 2024, the Court of Appeal published their judgment in relation to issues raised in the appeal bid by Lucy Letby's legal team. The remit of an appeal is quite narrow. You can't just throw in dozens of theories or arguments (of which there are many) as to why Letby might be innocent. In order to win the right to appeal, Letby's team had to prove that the trial made mistakes. The other way to win an appeal would be to present brand new evidence which cast serious doubt on the conviction. Ben Myers KC attempted to do both of these things. The applicant wanted all the evidence by Dr Dewi Evans, the chief prosecution witness, to be disregarded. Letby's legal representatives believed he was not an impartial witness and also questioned his expertise. In particular, the diagnosis of air embolism as a cause of death (or possible cause) in several of the infants by Dr Evans was, argued the defence, based on faulty evidence. Letby's defence team further argued that Dr Evans had no expertise when it came to air embolism.

An air embolus, also known as air embolism, occurs when air bubbles enter the bloodstream and can block blood vessels. This can lead to serious complications, as the air bubbles can obstruct blood flow to vital organs. Prevention of air embolism relies on careful surgical techniques, proper patient positioning, and vigilant monitoring during invasive procedures. Healthcare professionals are trained to avoid the risk of air entering the bloodstream, employing measures like airtight seals in intravenous lines and ensuring adequate control of pressures during invasive practices. Air embolisms are not obvious in post-mortems in the way that something like, for example, an infection or injury would be. Dr Evans argued (in his interviews after the trial) that this is why evidence of foul play did not seem to be obvious to pathologists. This has become a common theme for those who don't believe Letby is guilty or are unconvinced by the prosecution case at the trial. They point to the fact that none of the post-mortems talked about serial killers or air embolisms and that only happened when Dr Evans turned up. The issue, like everything in the Letby case, was more complex though. In some cases there were no immediate post-mortems because the parents (who obviously had no idea about foul play allegations at the time) didn't want that to happen.

In court at the original trial, Mr Myers had even appeared to question Dr Evans expertise as a neonatologist - pointing out that he hadn't been in clinical practice for a long time. Mr Myers also pointed out during the trial that Dr Evans had become interested in the Lucy Letby case and contacted the Cheshire Police offering himself as a medical expert. The implication then was that Dr Evans was 'touting' for work and saw the Lucy Letby case as some sort of gravy train. It was true that Dr Evans had offered his services but how did this make him impartial? If he had found no evidence of foul play at the hospital he surely would have said so to the police. Are we to believe that Dr Evans pretended Lucy Letby was a serial killer just to give himself some extra work? The main thrust of the appeal was that Dr Evans was incompetent and had come up with conclusions to fit his fanciful hypothesis. Dr Evans was the not the only person the police employed though. The work of Dr Evans for the prosecution was peer reviewed by Dr Sandie Bohin.

Dr Bohin was the Head of Neonatology at University Hospitals Leicester for seven years. She now works as a paediatrician in Guernsey. Dr Bohin more or less agreed with the conclusions of Dr Evans in her report. Some supporters of Lucy Letby have painted them as two peas in a pod and suggested that Dr Bohin merely parroted whatever Dr Evans concluded. In the summer of 2024, Dr Michael Hall wrote a letter to the British

Medical Journal in which he was critical of Dr Evans and Dr Bohin and appeared to question their suitability to be medical experts for the police in the Letby case. 'The verdict following the retrial of Baby K followed soon after the announcement by the Appeal Court judges,' wrote Dr Hall, 'on 2nd July 2024, that all applications for leave to appeal the convictions in the original 2023 trial were refused. The trial jury would have been aware of this decision and it is possible it influenced them in reaching their verdict. The judgement raises important issues concerning the interface between the legal and medical professions with regard to evaluation of medical and scientific evidence and the regulation of expert witnesses.

'The phrase "skin discolouration" appears 48 times in the judgement; the names "Lee and Tanswell" appear 25 times. A major component of the prosecution case was that the skin discoloration observed in some of the babies who were the alleged victims of Lucy Letby was caused by her injecting air into their veins, leading to "air embolism". The main medical evidence offered by the prosecution in support of this accusation was a paper by Lee and Tanswell which reviewed 53 published cases of neonatal "air" embolism.(1) Certain types of skin discoloration were reported in some of the cases. After reviewing this evidence, the judges concluded that any form of skin discoloration may be a sign of air embolism, provided that it is not the only clinical sign. The judges did not list the other signs but sudden unexpected collapse seems to be one of them.

'The basis for the judges' determination is flawed, in my opinion, for the following reasons: (i) The Lee and Tanswell paper, despite its misleading title, did not describe features of air embolism – the gas which entered the babies' circulation was primarily oxygen, not air, and it was pumped at high pressure into the pulmonary circulation, not injected into a peripheral vein. (ii) I have found only one paper which describes specific skin changes associated with the accidental injection of air, rather than oxygen, into a peripheral vein.(2) The changes were quite different to those described by Lee and Tanswell and to those described in the trial babies. Of particular note, the changes were not transient or "migratory", a pivotal feature of the case alleged by the prosecution and embraced by the judges.

'It is likely that an independent experienced medical reviewer would have identified these evidential concerns and would have been able to advise the judges accordingly. The second issue relates to the suitability of the two prosecution neonatal expert witnesses to interpret for the Court neonatal practice as it was in 2015-2016. Dr Evans had retired from full-time clinical practice in neonatal intensive care in 2009 and Dr Bohin also in 2009, although she continued to practise in Guernsey as a consultant paediatrician with neonates – that is in each case 13 years before the start of the trial.

'In all, five judges determined that the two expert witnesses were suitably qualified to give evidence and that it was for the jury to assess the validity of their evidence. But, first, on what basis were the judges qualified to make this decision? Second, as no medical expert witnesses were called for the defence, how could the jury assess the validity of the prosecution medical expert evidence, in the absence of any peer comparators offered by the defence? There is a need to explore how we – the medical and legal professions - can do better in combining our areas of expertise in the identification and evaluation of medical evidence. In the meantime, we need to recognise and respect the boundaries of our different areas of expertise.'

This letter inevitably came to the attention of Dr Bohin and as you might expect she did not take too kindly to it. She drafted a response for the BMJ to publish. 'I wish to address,' wrote Dr Bohin, 'some misleading and untrue comments about me and my suitability to be a medical expert in this case. I am accredited in neonatology and from 1996-2009 worked as a consultant in a tertiary centre neonatal unit. From 2009 I have worked in Guernsey undertaking both paediatric and neonatal work, including neonatal intensive care. I also have an honorary contract with a regional neonatal intensive care unit in the UK. I continue to work full time in clinical practice, unlike Professor Hall who retired from clinical work in 2018, long before the Letby trial came to court. Those who instructed me were clearly satisfied that I had the necessary expertise to act as an expert. It is wrong of Professor Hall to publicly discredit a professional colleague in this way. I'm not entirely sure of his motive. Is it a case of sour grapes because he was not called by the defence to take the stand? It certainly appears that way.'

Dr Bohin, who obviously gave evidence at the original trial, was also mentioned in the appeal bid. Letby's team claimed that Dr Bohin had given 'inconsistent evidence' when it came to air embolism and had admitted there wasn't much literature on the subject. The subtext of this complaint then was that Dr Bohin was admitting that she didn't know much about the subject. The appeal bid mentioned several other medical experts who had given evidence at the trial and argued that they too had no expertise when it came to an air embolism. Letby's defence team also wanted new evidence by Dr Shoo Lee to be considered. Dr Shoo Lee, a neonatologist and co-author of a paper called Pulmonary Vascular Air Embolism in the Newborn, gave evidence at the appeal and had issues with some of the prosecution evidence at the trial in relation to air embolism. Letby's defence team had high hopes for Dr Lee's intervention but it didn't turn out to be the game changer they might have wished. One problem with the defence position was it sounded a lot like they were arguing that no one in the world apart from Dr Lee and Dr Hall knew anything about diagnosing air embolisms.

At the trial, the prosecution had used some of Dr Lee's work in relation to their claim that Lucy Letby had injected air into some of the infants. The defence had now produced Dr Lee in person (well, by video link from Canada) to dispute whether his research had been applied correctly. It was, the defence hoped, their ace trump card in this appeal. However, Dr Shoo Lee had to concede that he had not read the medical records in relation to the infants in the case and was not up to speed with the witness statements given by medical staff and experts at the trial. The prosecution argued that this made Dr Lee's intervention pointless because his lack of knowledge in relation to the infant medical records and statements given during a marathon ten month trial made him wholly unqualified to be the driving component of an appeal. They painted Dr Lee as being rather like a man who had inserted himself into the middle of argument with no clear grasp on what exactly the argument was about.

The other problem for the defence is that it is often wrongly implied that Dr Evans and the prosecution relied entirely on the work of Dr Lee for their research on air embolisms. This was inaccurate. In his report on air embolisms for the criminal investigation, Dr Evans used eighteen different research papers and sources. So in reality Dr Lee's work made up a relatively small proportion (about 5%) of the research. Nick Johnson, for the prosecution, argued that the evidence of Dr Shoo Lee did not retrospectively call into question the outcome of the trial and that the defence was attributing things to the trial witnesses in relation to air embolisms which they did not actually say or mean. In the view of the prosecution, Dr Shoo Lee's new evidence did not contradict the evidence heard in court. In fact, the prosecution argued that the evidence at the trial fitted Dr Lee's research.

Mr Johnson suggested that if the defence placed such value on Dr Shoo Lee they should have called him as a witness at the trial. The Court of Appeal judgment echoed this and stated in their ruling that Ben Myers had been perfectly entitled to call Dr Lee as a witness at the trial but chose not to do so. Ben Myers disputed the scientific reliability of the air embolus theory which was used to explain several of the deaths in the hospital. Nick Johnson disagreed with these complaints and argued that the descriptions of skin discolouration on the infants was not, as Mr Myers claimed, a contradiction from established academic studies on the subject. This was the basic thrust of the debate on this issue. Much as he had done at the trial, Ben Myers placed most of his chips on Dr Evans and the air embolism theory as the most vulnerable part of the case. This was an understandable strategy because if it could be clearly proven that Dr Evans was barking up the wrong tree with his air injection diagnosis then the whole case against Lucy Letby is called into question and probably collapses. In the end the appearance by Dr Lee was all for nothing. It cut no ice with the Court of Appeal.

The Court of Appeal judgment ruled that grounds for fresh evidence had not been met and disagreed with the argument of Mr Myers that air embolism was scientifically dubious as an explanation for many of the deaths in this case. 'We do not accept that the level of scientific knowledge concerning air embolism is so limited that no reliable expert evidence at all can be given about it. Air embolus as a cause of collapse or death in a neonate is not a "bogus" medical theory. The fact that air embolus can occur in neonates is not in dispute. Research is necessarily limited, and the number of observed cases is fortunately small; and there are therefore limits to the extent of scientific knowledge of the topic. But it does not follow that there can be no expert evidence as to whether an air embolus did or did not occur in a particular case.'

The Court of Appeal also disagreed with the complaint that the chief prosecution medical witnesses were permitted to talk about areas in which they had no expertise. The judgment was that the medical witnesses in court had been conscientious and careful when it came to not straying into areas which were beyond their remit or specific area of expertise. During the trial, Mr Myers had pointed out that when Dr Evans had acted as a witness in a previous case he had been criticised by a judge for being impartial and making speculations which were outside his area of medical expertise. In response to this, Dr Evans had said this was the only judge who had criticised him during his thirty years in court as a medical witness. He said he had no idea that his report was going to be used in that case and only learned of the judge's comments years later. Dr Evans denied that he was a full-time 'prosecution witness' and said he never began a case with the goal of 'pointing the finger' at someone.

The Court of Appeal did not agree with the applicant when it came to criticisms of the expertise ad competence of Dr Evans. The judgment addressed this with the following paragraph - 'Dr Evans qualified as a medical practitioner in 1971. He trained in paediatrics in Swansea, then in Cardiff and Liverpool. Each phase of that training involved specific training in neonatology and working in a neonatal unit. He was appointed a full-time clinical consultant paediatrician in Swansea in 1980, a position he held until 2009. During the 1980s he became involved in the development of the new born services and intensive care services for babies. He was responsible for setting up, supervising and leading a neonatal intensive care service in Swansea from his appointment, developing intensive care services "from scratch." His experience was, he said, "very much hands-on." In 1990, in Swansea, the health board built a new children's department, which included a new neonatal unit which he helped to design. His operational and managerial roles involved serving as clinical director of paediatrics and neonatology in Swansea between 1992 and 1997, and between 2004 to 2008.'

Another complaint in the appeal was that the judge was wrong to direct the jury that they did not have to be sure of the precise harmful act or acts before they could convict on a particular count. The Court of Appeal ruled that the judge had been fair by expanding on this instruction and later telling the jury - "In the case of each child, without necessarily having to determine the precise cause or causes of their death, and for which no natural or known cause was said to be apparent at the time, you must be sure that the act of acts of the defendant, whatever they were, caused the child's death, in that it was more than a minimal cause. The defendant says that she did nothing inappropriate, let alone harmful to any child. Her case is that the sudden collapses and deaths were or may have been from natural causes or from some unascertained reason or from some failure to provide appropriate care and were not attributable to any deliberate harmful act by her."

Another issue raised by the applicant in the appeal was the court had been told, through an email, that a member of the jury was openly talking about the case in a cafe during breaks in the trial. The sender of the email claimed that the juror indicated the minds of the jury were already made up and they were always going to find Lucy Letby guilty. This was obviously a very serious charge and one that demanded investigation. If this was proven then Ben Myers had every right to complain about this. The authorities responded to the email more than once in order to question the sender and test the veracity of this claim. But they got no response. When they investigated the email address they found it was a new email account that had barely been used. They could not establish who the sender of this email was.

The conclusion of the appeal judgment was that this was possibly a 'crank' email sent by someone who wished to somehow help Lucy Letby or (even more bizarrely) may have been the result of an altercation over a phone transaction between the juror's wife and a cafe owner. The juror in question was not judged to have been at fault. His conduct at the trial was described as professional. Ultimately, this drama concerning the cafe and the email didn't really have much relevance to the question of whether Lucy Letby was a serial killer or not. The claim that the jury was always going to find Letby guilty doesn't have much basis in fact. They couldn't reach a decision on Child K, found Letby not guilty on some counts, and took a very long time to reach a decision on other convictions. It isn't as if they reached a verdict twenty minutes after the trial ended and demanded Letby be hanged. Who knows what might have happened if Dr Hall had given evidence? Dr Hall said this very thought gave him sleepless nights.

Lucy Letby will not be able to mount endless appeals though she may have the option of the Criminal Cases Review Commission (CCRC). The only way she could prove her innocence would be if fresh evidence came to light which was compelling enough to make her convictions unsafe. But where is this game changing evidence? Ben Myers has never managed to find it. In September, 2024, Letby hired a new barrister in the form of Mark McDonald. McDonald compared the Lucy Letby case to the Guildford Four and Birmingham Six and said it was one of the greatest miscarriages in history. Mr McDonald certainly talked a good game and said he was confident it could proven that the medical evidence at the trial of Lucy Letby was unreliable. McDonald specialises in criminal defence and founded the London Innocence Project (which operates to exonerate the wrongfully convicted). He was no stranger to trying to clear convicted medical killers because he represents Ben Geen. Geen was a nurse convicted of killing two of his own patients and committing grievous bodily harm against 15 others while working at Horton General Hospital in Banbury in 2003 and 2004.

McDonald also represents Michael Stone - who was convicted of the 1996 murders of Lin and Megan Russell and the attempted murder of Josie Russell. It is claimed by McDonald that Levi Bellfield confessed to these murders in prison - though the jury is still out on how valid that confession was. Mark McDonald has described Michael Stone as a good friend.

This is a slightly odd thing for a barrister to say about a client who has other convictions for robbery, burglary, grievous bodily harm and assault occasioning actual bodily harm. Stone has beaten up girlfriends, robbed people by spraying ammonia in their face, and stabbed more than one person. He definitely isn't someone you'd want living next door to you. Even if you take away the Russell case, Stone is still suspected of other murders. Mark McDonald was tweeting about Lucy Letby's innocence before the ink was even dry on the court convictions. He appears to be highly dubious when it comes to convictions against medical killers. McDonald's social media history is full of posts relating to the dire state of the NHS so one can probably see where he is coming from on the Letby case in his belief that care failings were to blame.

Mark McDonald opined that the reason why the defence in

Lucy Letby's trial didn't call any medical witnesses is that doctors are very reluctant to get involved in cases where there is abuse or harm to a child. When asked if it was a mistake to put Letby in the witness box, McDonald said that barristers have to think very hard about that and only tend to put the suspect in the witness box if they think it will help. Mr McDonald stated that, in his view, Letby's poor performance in the witness box was not a sign of guilt because anyone in that situation would find it difficult and not be able to remember everything or answer every question. McDonald said the defence couldn't win because if they hadn't put Letby in the witness box this might not have gone over well with the jury. In this scenario one could venture that Ben Myers KC took the least worst option.

THIRWALL

The ongoing Thirlwall Inquiry was set up to report on what happened at the Countess of Chester Hospital when Lucy Letby was working there. Why was the process of removing Letby from duty and bringing in the police so agonisingly slow? Why was the hospital management so reluctant to take any action? Before the inquiry had even begun, a private letter signed by 24 'experts' was sent to the government asking them to postpone the inquiry or alter its remit. The letter mentioned 'possible negligent deaths that were presumed to be murders' - which indicated the position of these experts was that they didn't believe Letby's convictions were safe. 'While we acknowledge the gravity of the convictions against Ms Letby, our focus is on the broader implications for patient safety, healthcare management, and the potential for miscarriages of justice in complex medical cases. We believe that legal systems are particularly vulnerable to errors when dealing with intricate scientific evidence, especially in cases involving statistical anomalies in healthcare settings, and the complex physiology of neonates.'

The group of experts stressed they had no connections to Letby's defence team and were not seeking to relitigate the case. Or were they? They were clearly intent on undermining the inquiry and their letter included a request for an 'examination' of what happened at the hospital 'without the presumption of criminal intent'. Which is another way to say they thought Lucy Letby was innocent. One of the signatories of the letter was a statistician named Peter Elston. Elston certainly wasn't agnostic about Letby's convictions. His Twitter feed consists of little else but endless posts about Letby's innocence. Aside from the inevitable brigade of statisticians, the letter did at least have some professional medical figures. These included Dr Tariq Ali, the former head of the paediatric critical care unit at Oxford university hospitals, consultant neonatologist Dr Neil Aiton, Dr Neela Shabde, a consultant paediatrician and former clinical director of child health for north-east England, and neonatal intensive care nurse Jenny Harris. The signatories also included the forensic scientist Professor Gillian Tully CBE.

The inquiry was chaired by Lady Justice Thirlwall and took place at Liverpool Town Hall. The remit of the inquiry was not to examine the safety of Letby's convictions but to scrutinise what happened in the hospital and how these things were allowed to happen. Lady Justice Thirlwall was Dame Kathryn Mary Thirlwall, DBE. She practised as a barrister from 1982, was a High Court judge from 2010, and was promoted to the Court of Appeal of England and Wales in 2017. "There has been a huge outpouring of comment from a variety of quarters on the validity of the convictions," said Lady Justice Thirlwall. "As far as I am aware it has come entirely from people who were not at the trial. Parts of the evidence has been selected and there has been criticism of the defence at the trial. All of this noise has caused enormous additional distress to the parents who have already suffered far too much. It is not for me to set about reviewing the convictions. The Court of Appeal has done that with a very clear result." The reason why this was called the Thirwall Inquiry and not the Lucy Letby Inquiry is that they didn't want any relatives of the infants who died who might be following this inquiry to constantly see Letby's name each time this inquiry was mentioned.

The inquiry had the ability to call witnesses to give evidence. The solicitor Tamlin Bolton, who represented the families of the infants who had died, said that all the online chatter about Letby being innocent was very upsetting for the families. The inquiry was not live-streamed - as some may have hoped. The reason for this was that the hospital objected. The lack of a live-stream was not welcomed by some KC's as they feared it would be grist to the mill for 'conspiracy theorists' who believed Letby had been stitched up and was innocent. We learned at the first day of the inquiry that Letby had studied the case of Beverly Allitt as part of her nurse training. Between February and April 1991, while working as a nurse, Allitt was responsible for the deaths of four children and the serious injury of several others. Allitt's actions involved administering insulin and other medications to induce medical crises in her young patients. She was arrested and charged with multiple counts of murder and attempted murder. In 1993, she was convicted and sentenced to 13 life terms in prison.

Counsel to the inquiry Rachel Langdale KC, in her opening statements, said that 'distressingly' the Letby case was Allitt all over again. Langdale also mentioned Harold Shipman and how he was much loved by friends, family, and even patients.

One might think that the Shipman case was open and shut in comparison to Letby and it was in a sense because Shipman was forging wills before patients died, but there were parallels in that when he was suspected of foul play some of his supporters set up a fund to help him fight the case. Shipman's wife never accepted his guilt and stood by him to the bitter end. No matter the killer or the case there will always be some who refuse to believe the conviction is safe. If the Shipman case had happened today there would inevitably be a statistician out there somewhere posting on his blog about how mathematical probability proved that dear old Harold was innocent and had been stitched up by a heartless and crooked health establishment.

One of the problems with the post-trial Lucy Letby circus (if we can use that term) is you now have experts going against experts. The people who gave evidence at the trial and advised the police and prosecution were not charlatans or impostors who had purchased fake medical degrees online. They were real doctors and professors. Medical professionals with years of experience. Some of the people now questioning the evidence and medical conclusions at the trial are also professionals with years of medical experience. Which set of experts are more valid? Who is right and who is wrong? It may be noted that the experts involved in the trial had access to more information than most of those looking in from the outside but this doesn't mean mean that reasoned medical objections from those qualified in such matters should be dismissed or not listened to. This is one of the problems with the online discourse relating to Letby. People tend to drift into echo chambers and cherry pick what they want to hear. If anyone expresses the 'wrong' opinion in the wrong place they tend to get jumped on and downvoted. So people become very entrenched. This is what we call confirmation bias. The official status of this case, whether Letby's supporters agree or not, is that she is guilty. Changing this reality is going to be a formidable challenge for any legal representatives who take on the Letby case.

Rachel Langdale KC said at the inquiry that after the death of Child C, the Countess of Chester Hospital was starting to become infamous in medical circles. One doctor told the police that if you worked in another hospital staff there would sometimes mention Chester as if it was some cursed place. Rachel Langdale KC said that a post-mortem for Child C had initially indicated a natural cause of death. Child D's cause of death was initially judged pneumonia with acute lung injury. Dr Sandie Bohin, who peer reviewed the work of Dr Evans for the police and prosecution and gave evidence at the trial, disagreed with this and judged that Child D's pneumonia was under control and she was stable at the time of death. It should be noted that when the police were called in to investigate the hospital they were split into different teams and allocated different babies to investigate. They did this independently of one another with no contact. The purpose of this was to make sure their conclusions were independent and not influenced by anything.

Dr Dewi Evans, who helped the police and was the chief prosecution witness, did not arrive on the scene with a brief to unmask a serial killer. He'd never even heard of Lucy Letby at the time. Dr Evans has been at pains since the trial to point out that he has acted as a witness for the defence many times and got prosecution medical cases thrown out before. Nonetheless, Dr Evans has remained a lightning rod for critics of the convictions and the evidence. He has, whether wisely or unwisely, continued to talk to the media since the trial and even seems willing to engage in debates with critics of both him and the verdict. The other experts who gave evidence at the trial seem to have remained silent - most likely out of respect for the families. Into this silent void some critics of the conviction have suggested these experts are silent because of doubts they might have about the case. That was not the case with Dr Sandie Bohin - who agreed to be interviewed for a Panorama special. Dr Bohin stood by her conclusions and evidence and said those questioning the convictions did not have access to all the information that she did.

Rachel Langdale KC told the inquiry on the first day that despite three infant deaths in two weeks the Countess of Chester Hospital did initiate any sort of investigation. This was, said Langdale, an opportunity missed. The inquiry then heard how reports and meetings concerning the spate of deaths in the neonatal unit often failed to appear or take place. There were instances where post-mortem examinations did not take place out of respect for the grieving parents. This meant that natural causes were initially attributed to some of the deaths later deemed by the criminal investigation to have been suspicious. This was later latched onto by some of Letby's supporters (that natural causes were initially cited) but the issue was complex. The inquiry then heard that the low blood glucose of Child F was not treated as a red flag at the hospital and no second test was undertaken because the situation resolved itself. A doctor did consider the possibility that someone had poisoned the child deliberately but then dismissed this as too ridiculous to even think about.

The insulin and c-peptide results for Child F, in hindsight, should have warranted further investigation. The C-peptide to insulin ratio test is a clinical laboratory test used to help evaluate the function of insulin production in the pancreas. A by-product of insulin production, C-peptide is released in equal amounts to insulin when proinsulin (the precursor to insulin) is converted into insulin. Measuring C-peptide levels can give insight into how much insulin the pancreas is producing. Ian Harvey, the hospital medical director at the time and now retired, said that had he been informed of Child F's insulin reading then prompter action would have been taken. He probably would say that now wouldn't he? The inquiry heard that death of Child I was the fifth death at the hospital in less than five months. A post-mortem recorded natural causes but Dr Gibbs at the Countess of Chester was baffled by the baby's death.

It was at this time that Dr Stephen Brearey began to have some suspicions about Lucy Letby. Dr Brearey noted that the deaths usually seemed to occur on the night shift. If these deaths were all from natural cause one would expect a more random and diverse spread of times in relation to these events. Dr Brearey suggested a meeting with neonatal unit manager Eirian Powell and Dr Jayaram but this meeting never happened. "I think we still need to talk about Lucy," Dr Brearey had said in an email to Dr Jayaram. There were though discussions and meetings in the end and Eirian Powell decided to put Letby on the day shift where there would be more staff to watch over her. Dr Brearey only learned of this later. Eirian Powell said that at this stage she had no suspicions about Lucy Letby and the switch of shifts was purely to make sure Letby had more supervision. It seems that Eirian Powell assumed that doctors were perhaps worried Letby might be making mistakes and questioning her competence as a nurse. The notion that Letby might be a Beverly Allitt style serial killer was not in Powell's orbit at all. That was preposterous. Eirian Powell was very fond of Lucy Letby.

The decision to move Letby to the day shift to have more supervision sounded good on paper but in reality there were no more staff on the day shift than the night shift so Letby's clinical practice had as much licence to go unchecked during the day as it had done at night. Letby would later be charged with attacking Child I and Child M during the day. She was also still permitted to work extra shifts at night - which defeated the object of placing her on the day shift. Rachel Langdale KC told the inquiry that if Letby was taken off nights due to concerns why was she permitted to work unsupervised during the day and then volunteer for night shifts? It didn't make any sense. Child L, like Child F, was judged to have been poisoned with insulin yet the hospital at the time seemed to make no connection between these two cases. Rachel Langdale KC told the inquiry that the Countess of Chester, despite the deaths, produced little in the way of reviews or reports. A spate of unusual deaths like this was supposed to be reported to the District and Regional Health Authorities but the hospital had failed to do this.

Alison Kelly was the senior manager in charge of nursing at the time these events were happening in Chester. Dr Brearey sent an email to Kelly in which, for the first time it seems, a link between Letby and the spate of infant deaths was suggested to a senior figure. Alison Kelly asked colleagues to look into the matter. Eirian Powell responded with an email which read - "There is no evidence whatsoever against LL [Lucy Letby] other than coincidence. LL works full time and has the Qualification in Speciality (QIS). She is therefore more likely to be looking after the sickest infants on the unit. LL also avails herself to work overtime when the acuity or unit is over capacity." Alison Kelly did not get any worrying feedback about Letby from the nursing staff (quite the opposite) but did nonetheless send an email to the hospital director Ian Harvey expressing the view that a 'wider review' might be sensible. A meeting was arranged in which Dr Brearey could express his concerns about Letby.

The Thirwall Inquiry heard that Eirian Powell defended Letby at this meeting and seemed irritated at any suggestion of a link between Lucy Letby and the infant deaths. Ian Harvey described the meeting as calm and said he didn't remember anyone making direct allegations against Letby. Mr Harvey said nothing was said to him at the meeting about Letby harming infants. "Had I been told that she had been seen doing anything that compromised the safety of any patient or that there was evidence of potential intentional harm being caused to any of the babies I would have immediately moved to have her suspended from the unit." Dr Brearey was not happy with the lack of action prompted by this meeting. He was critical of both Ian Harvey and Alison Kelly in his statements to the inquiry. Brearey claimed he made clear at the meeting that the only common link between the unexpected spate of deaths was Lucy Letby being on duty. Dr Brearey said that despite promises of a more thorough review no action was taken as a result of this meeting.

Brearey sent an email to other paediatric consultants and asked them to inform him if there were any incidents where infants collapsed unexpectedly. At a fresh meeting Dr Brearey said he made it clear that he believed a member of staff may be responsible for the alarming cluster of deaths and resuscitations the neonatal unit had experienced. The inquiry now moved to the collapse of Child N. Letby was later charged with attempting to murder this infant by thrusting his nasogastric tube down his throat. Alison Kelly and Ian Harvey both claimed they were not told about this collapse. The Thirwall Inquiry was not painting a very good picture of this hospital thus far. It appeared to be a place where no one knew what was going on and no one communicated to one another. A cynical reading of the evidence might entertain the possibility that Ian Harvey was exaggerating how little he knew to dodge too much blame. The families of the infants in this case were scathing about Mr Harvey in the aftermath of the original trial. They complained that when they tried to get answers at the time of the tragedies, Harvey (who swiftly retired in 2018 with a very nice pension pot knocking on for £2 million) either 'fobbed them off' or didn't reply to their letters. In response to this, Harvey said his ability to respond to the families at the time was constricted by the ongoing criminal investigation.

After the deaths of Child O and Child P, the duty executive Karen Rees was told by Karen Townsend (the Director of Urgent Care) that Dr Brearey and Dr Jayaram both suspected that Lucy Letby was deliberately harming infants. Despite this, Alison Kelly and Karen Rees did not remove Lucy Letby from duty because they judged there was insufficient evidence for these claims. They were also aware that Eirian Powell was staunchly in support of Letby. The inquiry heard that Dr Brearey phoned Karen Rees at home and asked for Lucy Letby to be taken off duty. No action was taken though and Letby remained on duty. The inquiry heard that Dr Brearey was becoming very frustrated by the hospital not appearing to take any action over the concerns he had raised. In an email, he ended by noting, "Just to confirm then, Ian [Harvey] and Alison [Kelly] are happy for LL to work on NNU in the same capacity as last week despite the paediatric consultant body expressing our concerns that this may not be safe and that we would prefer her not to have further patient contact."

In a statement to the inquiry, Ian Harvey said that at this time he wasn't quite sure what the issue with Lucy Letby was and assumed it was over her competence (as opposed to intentional harm). Lucy Letby, luckily for the hospital, had some days off due to her and took them. It was decided that when she came back she could resume her duties but only with supervision. This never happened in the end and she never went back to the neonatal unit. There was a flurry of emails between doctors over the mounting suspicion in the hospital and Ian Harvey requested that the emails should cease because action was being taken. Harvey's inquiry statement expressed regret for this because it came across as someone seeking to shut down concerns doctors had. The general picture the inquiry painted was one that most who have followed the Letby case were already reasonably familiar with. A small group of consultants developed suspicions about Lucy Letby but couldn't get the nursing bosses and hospital management to believe them. The main problem was the lack of conclusive evidence. Critics of the consultants would say they if they suspected patients were being harmed or were at risk they should have just gone straight to the police and bypassed all the hospital bureaucracy. The consultants tend to agree with that view today and wish they had done exactly this.

THIRWALL PART II

Ian Harvey still didn't bring in the police. What he did instead was instigate a hospital review of the deaths to be carried out by Dr Gibbs and a nurse. The review found six cases where there seemed to be no logical explanation for the death. The review suggested that Lucy Letby had duties involving four of these infants. A wider review of mortality rates in the neonatal unit was then undertaken by the hospital. The review noted that the rate of deaths was unusual - even allowing for the volume of patients. A similar volume of patients in the past had not seen a spike in deaths on this level. The review acknowledged that nurse staffing levels were not ideal but did not come to any conclusions on whether this was a factor in the moralities. The inquiry heard that Sian Williams (Deputy Director of Nursing) thought it was now time to bring in the police. Lucy Letby had been moved to a desk job at this time. Letby was not happy about this.

It may be noted that the unexpected collapses and deaths in the neonatal unit seemed to stop when Letby was moved to a desk job - though critics of Letby's conviction will ask about deaths and collapses which happened when Letby wasn't on duty in the larger timeframe. Emails from Karen Rees at this time indicate she was annoyed by Letby not being allowed to resume being a nurse. Rees stated in an email that 'unsubstantiated allegations' about letby had been made by doctors. The view of Karen Rees was that Letby should either go back to work as a nurse or they should call the police. This strange middle ground that Letby found herself in didn't make much sense to Rees. At this time, Lucy Letby was given assurances by the nursing staff that she had done nothing wrong and would be able to go back to work soon. This was in line with Ian Harvey's inquiry recollection that the doctors were suspicious of Letby while the nursing staff were supportive.

Rachel Langdale KC told the inquiry that "The deaths of two of the triplets, Child O and Child P, catapulted the issue of Letby and neonatal mortality to the top of the executive team agenda." The inquiry heard that Alison Kelly informed the Nursing and Midwifery Council that a nurse was under suspicion although stressed that no evidence was available at this time. The inquiry was told of two pieces of evidence which indicated that Ian Harvey was advised to call the police in June 2016. The police were not though called for some months. In his inquiry statement, Ian Harvey said he had no recollection of being advised to bring in the police in June 2016. Harvey's memory seemed to be almost as bad as that of Lucy Letby. The Royal College of Paediatrics and Child made recommendations to the hospital and so neonatologist Dr Jane Hawdon conducted an external review of the incidents at the Chester neonatal unit at this time. Dr Hawdon was asked to study five cases - Child O, Child A, Child P, Child D and Child I.

Dr Hawdon concluded that Child D's death could have been a result of antibiotics not being administered quickly enough. Dr Hawdon said the other cases were unexplained. Dr McPartland, a consultant paediatric pathologist based at Alder Hey Children's Hospital, was also asked to review four of the cases. She cited prematurity as a possible factor in two and said the other two were unexplained. Dr Hawdon's report was not permitted by the judge to be used as evidence in Lucy Letby's main original trial. A factor in this decision is that Dr Hawdon admitted she had only a few days to make her report so it wasn't extensive or exhaustive. Dr Hawdon said she was told nothing about allegations that a nurse was harming patients and had limited information to work on. Some supporters of Lucy Letby have used Dr Hawdon in their arguments that the babies died of natural causes or were not stable but like everything else in this case it was a lot more complicated than that. Dr Hawdon basically dismissed her own report so it was hardly going to be of much use in exonerating Lucy Letby. As we'll see later, Dr Hawdon was called to speak to the inquiry in person.

Dr McPartland was also not aware at the time that a nurse was suspected of being a common factor in the deaths and collapses. In her statement to the inquiry, Dr McPartland said she should have been told this information. The inquiry evidence so far indicated that the hospital management was trying its best to keep this all in house and not divulge too much information. The paralysis of the bosses was not helped by the schism between some of the doctors and the nursing staff. Some of the doctors were now openly suggesting that

Lucy Letby had deliberately harmed infants. The nursing staff on the other hand were baffled by the insinuations that 'nice Lucy' had done anything wrong. By this time, Lucy Letby had instigated a grievance procedure with the hospital in protest at being taken off the neonatal unit. She had meetings with executives in accordance with this process. The inquiry heard that one or both of Letby's parents would often come to these meetings with her. Letby was an only child and very close to her parents.

Tony Chambers, the then chief executive of the NHS trust, seemed to believe at the time that the grievance procedure had exonerated Lucy Letby and told her as much. He assured Letby she had the support of the trust. The Thirwall Inquiry statement by Chambers sort of denied this. Mr Chambers said he wouldn't have said she was exonerated. This was contradicted though by inquiry evidence which suggested this is exactly what Chambers had led Letby to believe. The grievance procedure was not an investigation into Lucy Letby but when the grievance was partly upheld the hospital management seemed to act as if this had cleared her of any suspicion. Letby's father was fuming over the fact that some of the doctors had accused his daughter of being a murderer. The consultants who had expressed suspicions about Letby were told they now owed her an apology. So they were forced to apologise to Letby. Dr Brearey and Dr Jayaram did not though participate in a suggested mediation process.

At this point the Sunday Times indicated to the hospital they were planning to write an article about the rash of deaths which had taken place there. That article would not have cast the hospital in a very good light so bosses were not too happy about this threat. Ian Harvey, in damage limitation mode, released a statement in which he said only two deaths at the hospital were so far unexplained. This statement contradicted internal and external review findings. Lucy Letby and her parents were told that a 'line' had been drawn in this case and there would be no criminal investigation. At the start of 2017, Letby sent an email to the neonatal staff saying she had been exonerated (which wasn't true) and would be back at work with them soon. No one corrected her on this email. To be fair to the staff, it seems no one actually knew what was going on. Had Letby been cleared? Was she a serial killer? Did some nasty doctor have a personal grudge against her? There was even a rumour in the hospital that Letby had rebuffed romantic interest from one of the doctors - leading to bad blood. This rumour wasn't true at all but in the absence of clarity some theoretical corridor gossip was probably inevitable.

The married doctor that Letby exchanged over a 1000 messages with and went on daytrips and lunches with was called Dr U in the inquiry to protect his identity. He was supportive of Letby during this period and she spoke to him of getting an observational placement at Alder Hey Children's Hospital in Liverpool. Observational placement, as the name indicates, is where a medical professional goes to a hospital and observes others working to improve their pool of knowledge. Frustrated by her desk job, Letby undertook some placements at Alder Hey. The inquiry noted that this was very bizarre given that Letby, vague and confused as the investigation might have been, was still under suspicion of harming patients. The inquiry heard that Letby was still also visiting the neonatal unit in Chester in person. On one occasion there was even tea and cakes in the unit to welcome Letby back. A nurse told the inquiry that Letby seemed in a bad mood at this tea party and didn't say very much.

It was only at the start of May, 2017, that the hospital chief executive Tony Chambers contacted Cheshire Police and requested that they investigate what had gone on in the neonatal unit. Rachel Langdale KC told the inquiry that were it not for the lobbying of senior consultants, Lucy Letby would have gone back to work as a nurse. The decision to call the police was prompted by consultants urging a more thorough review of the deaths deemed unexplained. They also wanted the scope of this review to be widened so that it included more infants who had died or collapsed at the hospital. The inquiry heard that Tony Chambers was worried that they didn't have enough evidence to go to the police. Ian Harvey also seemed to share this view but felt it would be the transparent thing to do. What may have prolonged the cold feet when it came to contacting the police was legal advice that the police (who have limited time, money, and resources thanks to years of government cuts) will only investigate a matter like this if there is sufficient evidence and if a criminal investigation does go ahead this is going to be very bad for the reputation of the hospital.

On April the 13th, 2017, Dr Hawdon told Ian Harvey that one unexplained death in a neonatal unit is unusual so to have more than one was 'suspicious' and needed an investigation. When the police were finally called in they were given a 22 page document by the hospital which had findings from work by Dr Hawdon plus Dr Subhedar and other consultants. Rachel Langdale KC told the inquiry that Dr Brearey and Dr Jayaram were treated poorly by the hospital in that their concerns about Letby were not taken seriously by the hospital for a time and then they were forced to apologise to Lucy Letby under threat of disciplinary action. At the next day of the inquiry, Nicholas de la Poer KC spoke about how the board committee of the Countess of Chester Hospital didn't have a single meeting about the rise in deaths or the drama and suspicion surrounding Lucy Letby - even while all of this was going on. There were private discussions though. Nicholas de la Poer said the board were told to accept the recommendation of the Royal College of Nursing and allow Letby back to work. Sir Duncan Nicholl, former chair of the board of directors at the Countess of Chester Hospital, said in his enquiry statement that he was 'misled' by Tony Chambers and Ian Harvey.

The inquiry then went on to hear how the families of the infants involved in the case felt the communication from the hospital was not very good when it came to keeping them up to date with what was happening. Nicholas de la Poer noted that the Nursing and Midwifery Council only suspended Letby after she had been charged - two years after they had been informed of complaints about her. The inquiry presented a complex picture of this tangle of health authorities and bodies. A steering group failed to notice that neonatal deaths had more than doubled compared to previous years. A member of staff who went to Risk and Safety with concerns about Lucy Letby was more or less told to go away. While this bureaucratic logjam was going on, doctors were referring to Letby as 'Nurse Death' in emails and conversation. The main theme of the inquiry was the hospital not abiding by NHS protocol - which states that any suspicious activity must be reported to the police promptly so it can be investigated.

Lucy Letby was interviewed by the Royal College of Paediatrics and Child Health (RCPCH) in the midst of this drama. In a private social media post, Letby said she was told off the record that she needed to start preparing a defence in case she was accused of anything. The inquiry also heard that Dr Ravi Jayaram contacted the British Medical Association to ask for advice and express his fears about Lucy Letby. The BMA apparently said he should not raise this matter in any grievance proceedings relating to Letby. The Thirwall Inquiry was building a growing picture of all these external agencies who seemed to offer only deaf ears rather than advice or action. The Royal College of Paediatrics and Child Health made two reports on Letby - one of which made no mention of the allegations against her. The case of Rebecca Leighton and Stepping Hill was mentioned as a cautionary tale when it came to jumping to quick conclusions or pointing the finger when it came to hospital deaths. Neither of the reports by the RCPCH recommended that the Chester hospital should call the police or even report these matters to other medical authorities.

The Thirwall Inquiry heard that the hospital in Chester was by now struggling to keep a lid on this story. Det Ch Supt Nigel Wenham from Cheshire Constabulary attended a Child Death Overview Panel in March 2017 and was concerned when he learned of the neonatal spike in deaths at the hospital. NHS England were also aware of the problems at the hospital and watching closely. The inquiry heard that Ian Harvey told NHS England that paediatricians were 'prejudiced' towards Letby and there was no firm evidence against her. In July 2018, Harvey was referred to the General Medical Council (GMC) by disgruntled doctors. Alison Kelly was also referred to regulators after Letby's conviction. Peter Skelton KC singled out Ian Harvey and Eirian Powell for particular criticism when he addressed the inquiry on the third day. He blamed the failings partly on "professional reticence, institutional secrecy, the demonisation of whistle-blowers, the growing schisms between the nurses and doctors, and doctors and executives".

Skelton also addressed the fact that there was a (seemingly growing) movement now (in 2024) which either had doubts about Letby's guilt or believed she was innocent. The inquiry heard that statistical evidence was not used to convict Letby so any statisticians out there constantly banging on about this case on their blog or Twitter/X, in the view of Mr Skelton, were howling up the wrong tree. Richard Baker KC, who represented some of families of the infants Letby was convicted of killing, told the inquiry that the guilty verdict was being 'arrogantly' ignored by those who had taken it upon themselves to insist that Letby was innocent. Mr Baker said that, contrary to conspiracy theories now abounding, the infants Letby was convicted of attacking were for the most part stable. Some of them were even ready to be taken home. Baker said that people have a tendency to assume that serial killers look like 'monsters' but in reality they often look 'banal' and ordinary. The inquiry portrayed Letby's supporters as naïve and ill informed.

It was Richard Baker KC who delivered the biggest bombshell yet to emerge from the inquiry. He said that Letby had two work placements at Liverpool Women's Hospital in 2012 and 2015. Baker said it since been established that incidents of endotracheal (breathing) tubes being dislodged happened on 40% of Letby's shifts during her work placements. "It is unusual, and you will hear that it occurs generally in less than 1% of shifts," said Baker. Coincidence? Lies, damn lies, and statistics? This was the first time that any evidence for Letby allegedly attempting to harm patients outside of Chester had been revealed. The audit was carried out by the hospital in Liverpool. The opposing Letby camps on the internet took from this what they wanted to take. Those who believe Letby is guilty saw it as yet more evidence that the convictions were safe. Those who believe Letby is innocent dismissed it as nonsense and queried the methodology of the statistics. It was business as usual in the court of cyberspace.

On the next day of the inquiry, Kate Blackwell KC spoke for the NHS managers. Blackwell said that the managers involved in the drama over complaints against Letby did not ignore concerns but didn't have the full range of information available to them at the time. Blackwell said that Letby often worked extra shifts and had specialist training that not all nurses shared. Because of this it wasn't deemed unusual for Letby to be present in the unit during a number of emergency situations because she was there an awful lot of the time. The general message of the fourth day was regret that the police hadn't been called in sooner. The purpose of the inquiry was to get to the bottom of failings in the health system and the hospital and make sure they were less likely to happen again. For those people who still insisted that Letby was innocent there wasn't much in this inquiry for them so far. All they could do was carp from the side-lines. The inquiry was not here to second guess Letby's guilt. Dr Dewi Evans wasn't going to be dragged in and grilled over his trial evidence. The inquiry insisted that this was all settled.

There was distressing evidence on day five from the mother of Child C. This is the infant who Letby was convicted of killing by air embolism. The mother of Child C was scathing of Ian Harvey and also spoke of how Letby had tried to put the infant in a cold cot before it had even died. A cold cot is where deceased infants are placed so the family can have one more period with them. The mother of Child C told the inquiry that Lucy Letby was not the assigned nurse for her child but acted as if she was. The mother of Child D also gave evidence to the inquiry the next day. She said she was confused by the death of her child at the hospital because tests had indicated the infant was stable and getting much better. The mother of Child D revealed that she had written to Cheshire coroner Nicholas Rheinberg and demanded a full investigation because she was not satisfied with the answers (or lack of them) given by the hospital. An independent consultant paediatrician had advised the coroner that the death was unexplained and unexpected. Nicholas Rheinberg was asked to assess the deaths of several babies by the hospital but declined, complaining that the coronial service was not a quality assurance service for the NHS. He retired in 2017.

The mother of Child D told the inquiry that she found Lucy Letby's presence in the hospital made her feel uncomfortable and uneasy. She said Letby would keep appearing and stare at her. The mother of Child F, by contrast, noted in her evidence how friendly Letby was. She said Letby would hug her and seemed genuinely upset by events in the unit. The mother said, in hindsight, this was odd behaviour for a serial killer. The evidence given by the mothers was awful to have to listen to. The mother of Child E said she blamed herself for what had happened. Lady Thirwall told the mother that she was not to blame. The parents of Child G told the inquiry that they only found out why their child died during the trial of Lucy Letby. They said the hospital never explained anything to them at the time. At the trial the parents learned that their baby had been overfed with milk and suffered a head injury too. One mother said she always had a negative impression of Lucy Letby. "I didn't particularly like Lucy Letby. To me she looked miserable and she did not look like she enjoyed her work. I just thought she was not very good at her job." It was announced around this time that Letby was going to appeal her last conviction (the Child K retrial). The chances of this appeal being successful were remote indeed. Her new barrister Mark McDonald was going to have to play the long game.

THIRWALL PART III

The parents who gave evidence at the inquiry didn't have anything nice to say about the hospital managers. Some of them were even critical of the nurses too. A common theme was their complaint about lack of communication from the hospital as to what was happening to their babies. Some of them said they felt it should be standard practice to install CCTV in neonatal units. The trial of Lucy Letby certainly would have been a lot easier if they'd had a raft of CCTV tapes to consult. The reason why they don't have CCTV in hospitals to spy on patients and staff 24/7 is obviously due to privacy. If you are giving birth or breastfeeding or saying goodbye to a dying relative you don't really want a camera there filming everything. Some people don't think it would have made much difference anyway. If she really was a serial killer it seems unlikely that Lucy Letby would have been stupid enough to harm patients in full view of the cameras. She would presumably have found a way around this.

Professor Mary Dixon-Woods, from the University of Cambridge, gave evidence to the inquiry and spoke about how the first person to raise suspicions about Beverly Allitt was basically ignored because the hospital found the allegations of a serial killer nurse absolutely ludicrous. Dixon-Woods said the danger for the health service was to refuse to believe that people like Allitt and Harold Shipman are possible or even exist. A good chunk of the early part of the inquiry concerned safeguarding and what prevention measures could be put in place in the health system. On the 14th day of the inquiry there was evidence by Dr John Gibbs. Gibbs is a retired consultant paediatrician who worked at the Countess of Chester Hospital when Letby was a nurse there. Dr Gibbs told the inquiry he was 'ashamed' that he didn't do more to protect the patients from Lucy Letby.

Dr Gibbs said that Letby first attracted suspicion from some doctors in the hospital because she always seemed to be on the scene when a resuscitation had to be performed due to an emergency. Dr Gibbs told the inquiry that he didn't immediately suspect Letby himself because he assumed she was having a run of bad luck. He told the inquiry that all doctors and nurses have experienced a terrible period where they lose patients but these things tend to even out in the end. Things never did seem to 'even' out for Letby though. It might be noted at this point that the neonatal unit at Chester has apparently experienced one death in seven years since Lucy Letby left. It stopped taking new-borns for a time after Letby left and also underwent improvements and building work. Those who believe Letby is innocent would cite these factors for why the neonatal unit seemed to be no longer cursed anymore once Letby was gone. Dr Gibbs said he did not see the insulin reading for Child F himself and noted it as something which was missed (in that it did not seem to provoke a deeper investigation or alarm) by the hospital. Gibbs said that doctors, in hindsight, should have bypassed the hospital management and gone to the police.

Dr Gibbs told the inquiry that he began to have concerns about Letby after the death of Child I (who Letby was convicted of poisoning with insulin). He acknowledged that there were some care failings in the hospital but said these failings, in his professional view, were not significant enough to have been responsible for any of the deaths attributed to Letby. Dr Gibbs said what stopped him from escalating the situation at the time was knowledge of things like Stepping Hill (where the innocent Rebecca Leighton was wrongly charged with harming patients) and also the fact that the senior nurse dismissed the allegations against Letby and insisted that Lucy Letby was very competent and professional. After he agreed to inquiry questioning that he had come to regard Letby as a threat to safety, Dr Gibbs was asked why he not gone to the police himself. He replied by saying that he allowed himself to become guided by the opposition put up by the nursing staff. Dr Gibbs added that no post-mortems or eyewitness evidence seemed to back up any of the grave allegations against Letby.

Dr Rachel Lambie, a former paediatric registrar at the Countess of Chester Hospital, gave evidence on day 15. Dr Lambie disputed some of the evidence Letby gave at the trial concerning specific details but the main headlines from this day of the inquiry came from Dr Lambie's revelation that when the spike in deaths occurred in the unit she found the nurses all grouped around a computer studying the duty rota. What the nurses were doing was trying to work out if there was a nurse who was working all the shifts when these things happened. The nurses were basically doing some detective work to see if there was a potential Beverly Allitt (or simply an incompetent or unlucky nurse) among them. Dr Lambie said there was a strange and horrible atmosphere in the unit - especially on the night shifts where the emergencies had often occurred. She said she almost dreaded going in to work. It was a very weird and unusual situation at the hospital with the dark whispers against Letby and the nursing staff remaining in full support of their nurse. The consultants and nursing staff were pulling in different directions while the management looked on and tried to avoid becoming involved. Somewhere in the midst of this was Lucy Letby, her fate now on ever shifting sands. At times she must have felt like the worst was over but in reality the nightmare was only just beginning.

More than one doctor at the Thirwall Inquiry mentioned that they did consider the possibility of an infection or bug in the hospital but found no evidence for this theory. The superbug or infection theory is quite popular among a section of those who insist Letby is innocent. Dr Murthy Saladi told the inquiry that filters were put on the taps because he feared pseudomonas (a type of bacterium that can cause serious infections) but no evidence for the superbug theory was established. Dr Elizabeth Newby, who worked on the neonatal unit at the Countess of Chester hospital, told the inquiry that a bug or possible contamination of equipment was considered as a possibility for the deaths and this was investigated with some extra preventative measures put in place. There was though no medical evidence of infection. If there was they would have picked that up quite easily according to doctors who worked at the hospital.

Dr Huw Mayberry, another paediatric registrar at the Countess of Chester Hospital when Letby worked there, told the inquiry that Letby taking home so many handover notes struck him as highly unusual. Hospital staff are instructed to put handover notes in the bin when they finish a shift because they contain confidential medical information. Dr Mayberry said he was bewildered at the time by the deaths of Child O and Child P because there was nothing to indicate they were in danger. The possibility that a member of staff might be doing this was not something he considered at this time. Dr Mayberry said he was dubious about CCTV in hospitals because it would be possible to harm a patient without the camera picking this up and thus might give hospitals a false sense of assurance. Dr Cassandra Barrett told the inquiry that she had referred to Lucy Letby as 'Nurse Death' to other staff members at the hospital but said this was gallows humour due to Letby always seeming to have bad things happen on her shifts. Dr Barratt said she didn't actually suspect Letby of anything at the time.

Dr Suzy Holt, who worked at the hospital when Letby was there, told the inquiry she was embarrassed that doctors (including her) were forced to sign a letter of apology to Letby. Dr Holt also seemed to be irritated by the way the hospital was depicted as some failed institution riddled with incompetence. Dr Holt felt that the hospital in Chester had offered good care to patients. Dr Elizabeth Newby told the inquiry that an air of 'disbelief' stopped doctors from taking action (calling the police) independently because they couldn't quite get their heads around the enormity of what they suspected. A theme of the evidence was that hospital executives were desperate to avoid calling the police if they could because of the negative publicity it would generate for the hospital. The executives placed their faith and hope in the fact that the nursing staff seemed to be supporting Letby as a counter to the concerns of some of the doctors. "We now know that she has been tested in a court of law and found guilty," said Dr Holt, "but at that time we were still dealing with uncertainty. Can this possibly be true?"

On day 17 of the inquiry there was evidence from the registrar who worked at the hospital and exchanged over a 1000 text and email messages with Letby during this time. They are said to have gone on a daytrip together and their private messaging indicated a lot of affection. The doctor in question (who was married with children) had his identity protected at Lucy Letby's trial and when he gave evidence to the inquiry this privacy was continued and he was identified only as Dr U. Dr U had been instrumental in Letby getting a placement elsewhere at a time when she was under growing suspicion in Chester. The inquiry seemed to establish that when she got a placement in Liverpool, the hospital there had no idea that Letby was currently suspected of harming patients in Chester - which is a remarkable state of affairs. It was this doctor who had caused Letby to become emotional when he gave evidence at her trial. Dr U was asked why he seemed to support Letby at a time when the other doctors were expressing doubts about her. He said that he was concerned about Letby's mental health and was helping her get through a difficult period. Dr U said that, in hindsight, he was manipulated and misled and had regrets. Like some of the nursing staff and much of the management, he found the notion that Leby was a serial killer hard to believe. Dr U said that he wasn't aware of the 'full clinical picture' at the time and didn't know what the full extent of the allegations against Letby were.

A paediatrician, who also remained anonymous and gave evidence as 'Dr UZ', told the inquiry that hospital bosses stuck their heads in the sand when it came to Letby and wanted them (the doctors) to shut up and stop talking about her. Dr UZ said she deeply regretted not taking action over the insulin cases but saw the test result too late to make an immediate medical deduction of foul play (by that she meant the baby in question had normal readings by the time she saw the original test). Dr UZ said she got the impression from meetings with the management that her job would be at risk if she didn't stop expressing concerns about Letby. Dr UZ said this was something she had to take seriously because she had a mortgage and bills to pay. She couldn't afford to be suddenly unemployed. There was evidence during this part of the inquiry that the deaths occurred on days when the hospital was generally well staffed and not experiencing any chronic shortage of nurses. One other detail which seemed to emerge was evidence that Letby was on shift when all but one of the deaths occurred.

Dr Sean Tighe, of the British Medical Association (BMA), gave evidence the next day and told the inquiry that the hospital bosses in Chester were dictatorial in the way they tried to gag doctors over their concerns regarding Letby. Dr Tighe said that he did have some sympathy with the management in that they were trying to observe some sort of fair process and had no firm evidence against Letby to act upon. He felt it was inappropriate though that a 'melodramatic' statement from

Letby was read out at one of the meetings. In the statement, Letby said, 'My life was turned upside down and subsequently put on hold, when I was unexpectedly informed, in July 2016, that I was being redeployed from the Unit following a period of annual leave. I have not entered the Unit since. There has been a huge element of dishonesty throughout this process and I want to ensure that you all hear my perspective and are aware of the impact your actions have had on me.

'I appreciate that we all have a right to raise concerns, and that the protection of our vulnerable patient group, is, of course, of paramount importance. However, I find it extremely unprofessional and hurtful to have been made aware of such unsubstantiated insensitive comments, as listed below, often via 'word of mouth'. Some of these were voiced in public areas / meetings. It was only through the submission of my grievance that all of these 'comments' were confirmed. It was suggested by some of the Paediatric Consultants that the link (my presence on the unit and the increased mortality rates) "was due to a knowingly deliberate action by LL". It has been noted that "Consultants were not prepared to have me on the unit" and that "as a team you continued to apply pressure to have me removed" "If I were not removed, the police would be called" "Consultants were uncomfortable that I would be on the unit" and wanted me "suspended".

'Members of your team have been heard to publicly make comments such as 'Angel of death', 'murderer on the unit', 'cold and calculated' A member of the Consultant team, when asked how they would feel if I were to kill myself or if something were to happen to my elderly parents (Letby was exaggerating a little bit here as her mother Susan was still in her fifties at the time) as a result, has been documented as replying "I do not care". No individual and certainly no parent should have to hear something as distressing as this. As concluded by my grievance report which states "It is clearly evident from the witness statements that your movement from the unit was orchestrated by consultants with no hard evidence to support this action." I was also disappointed to have discovered within my grievance that analysis tables relating to the morality rates had columns 'amended' by your team with information relating to the involvement of medical staff being 'removed.'

'Due to my professionalism/dedication/commitment/work ethic I have exceeded expectations in my new role and remained in work, despite time off being suggested by numerous people on many occasions. The reason for remaining in work being that I am completely innocent of all verbal allegations made against me which has been confirmed within my grievance report. In some ways, time off may have been easier than having to constantly walk past the Women and Children's building knowing that I could not enter for fear of seeing any of you or bumping into colleagues and having to lie. The isolation from friends and colleagues since July has been huge and I am yet to see if it has any lasting impact on my team relationships The unit is a small, close knit team with some members also being friends. Having to limit contact with them and be under the pretence of a voluntary secondment has resulted in my support network being extremely restricted.

'The secrecy of this situation has been, in my opinion, to protect you more than it was to benefit me - I have never had anything to hide. I therefore wish to be as open and honest as possible with my colleagues pending my return and I will be releasing a statement. I feel they have the right to know the truth behind my secondment and restricted contact, which is very out of character for me. I hope this will also enable relationships to be rebuilt and for me to be supported in my return to the team. After working with you all in a professional and supportive manner during difficult and challenging times I have been hurt and disappointed that those of you who did not openly raise concerns felt unable to be more supportive of me in this situation. The detrimental effect this has had on me, my family, and potentially my future is immense.

'Many months of worry, distress, secrecy and uncertainty has had a significant impact on my physical health, general wellbeing and self-confidence. I am not the person I was before this began. It is only now that there is some light at the end of the tunnel that I feel as though I can start to try to become the person I was before. A lot of people would leave/ move on/ have a fresh start and I know that is the feeling which has been conveyed to me by some of you "the longer she is away from the unit, the more likely she will be to leave", however, I am very passionate about and dedicated to Chester - it is where I undertook my nurse training and the unit helped me to grow from a student to a newly qualified nurse and beyond. Although this has been very traumatic, my strong desire to remain in Chester and within CoCH remains, and I am hopeful that we can find a professional way forward to enable my return to where I feel I belong.'

Dr Tighe said he later got an impression that one of the parents of the children who died had threatened to complain to the General Medical Council (GMC) over allegations against Letby. Dr Tighe said this was the nuclear deterrent for a doctor or administrator because if you were referred to the GMC it was disastrous for your career. Dr Paul Jameson, chair of the hospital's medical staff committee, told the inquiry that doctors were frustrated by their inability to get the hospital action over Letby and also felt threatened by the fact that complaints against Letby appeared to be potentially hazardous to their careers. Dr Michael McGuigan said he was advised by Tracy Bullock, the chief executive of Leighton Hospital in Crewe, that care failings were responsible for the incidents in Chester and if doctors continued to cling to the serial killer nurse theory then that wouldn't end very well for their careers. The inquiry heard that Stephen Cross, the Chester hospital's director of legal services and head of corporate affairs, was against calling the police because he feared it would mean the end of the neonatal unit at the hospital.

Obstetrician Dr Jim McCormack told the inquiry he was rather bemused to have to write a letter of apology to Lucy Letby despite not having the faintest idea who she was. Dr McCormack had asked other doctors if they suspected there was a 'murderer' in the hospital and because he used the word 'murderer' he was forced to apologise to Letby despite not mentioning her by name or even knowing who she was at the time. Kathryn de Beger, who was Letby's occupational health manager, told the inquiry she exchanged about 750 messages with Letby. Kathryn de Beger's job was to provide support to Letby and give her someone to confide in and talk to. Kathryn de Beger said that Letby was very hurt by the allegations against her and troubled by the tragedies in the neonatal unit. Kathryn de Beger told the inquiry she had told Letby that going to Liverpool on placement would be good for her. Asked why she was suggesting this during a time of grave allegations against Letby, Kathryn de Beger said she assumed this placement had been put in place by senior managers. Asked if she believed the allegations against Letby at the time, Kathryn de Beger replied by saying this was not her 'remit' and her duty was merely to provide Letby with support.

Neonatal Assistant Elizabeth Marshall told the inquiry she thought it was odd that Letby always seemed to be involved in the care of the babies who fell ill and odder still that after a death Letby always declined the offer of time off and insisted on going back to Nursery one with the more special care infants. Marshall, while conceding that this fell into the realm of circumstantial evidence at the time, said she did find it unusual and even vaguely suspicious the way that Letby never need time off to 'regroup' after a death in the way that most staff would. Elizabeth Marshall described Letby as a very 'closed off' person with a very high opinion of her own medical expertise. Kathryn Percival-Calderbank, who was a senior nurse at the hospital when Letby was there, conceded to the inquiry that there sometimes staffing shortages which made it difficult during busy periods. Percival-Calderbank said Letby was irritated and angry when she was told to take a break from Nursery one and later just went back in there anyway.

Kathryn Percival-Calderbank said she had a 'niggle' that something was amiss in the neonatal unit but she never for a moment suspected foul play might be a factor. Ashleigh Hudson, who was a neonatal nurse alongside Letby at the hospital, said to the inquiry that the unit was not understaffed. Hudson said that nurses underwent training to spot terrorists but didn't really do any training to spot serial killers on the ward. Nurses told the inquiry that there was a module on Beverly Allitt as part of their training but it was quite brief and they usually forgot most of it anyway by the time they started working. Ashleigh Hudson said she was annoyed when Letby sent her a text saying that Child A had died. Hudson felt a text was not the appropriate way to impart this information and also breached patient/family privacy. Another nurse, named Melanie Taylor, told the inquiry that she had wanted to move Child O back to Nursery one but Letby had said the infant should stay in Nursery two. Taylor said she regretted she hadn't been more firm with Letby because the infant seemed poorly to her and Nursery one was better equipped for poorly infants. Taylor said, in light of Letby's convictions, there was a potential motive here from Letby to ponder in hindsight.

Melanie Taylor said that she recalled one occasion where Letby told her about the death of a baby in a weird way, as if this was exciting news or gossip which had to be shared straight away. Taylor said she found Letby 'strange' but unlike the doctors had no suspicions that she was harming patients. Melanie Taylor also told the inquiry that Letby was a very competent nurse who seemed good at her job. The nurses seemed to be some way behind the doctors when it came to learning about the allegations against Letby. The inquiry heard about the email Lucy Letby sent to her colleagues when she wrongly presumed she had been cleared and could put this matter behind her. 'I was redeployed from the Unit in July 2016 following serious and distressing allegations of a personal and professional nature made by some members of the medical team. From then until now I have been unable to visit or contact the Unit whilst these matters were investigated. After a thorough investigation it was established that all the allegations were unfounded and untrue and I have therefore been fully exonerated. I have received a full apology from the Trust but as you can imagine this whole episode has been extremely distressing for me and my family. I will begin my return to the Unit in the coming weeks. I will need colleagues to be sensitive and supportive at this time.'

The inquiry heard from (deputy ward manager on the hospital's children's unit) Nicola Lightfoot that Lucy Letby failed her final year student nurse placement. Lightfoot was Letby's assessor when this happened. Letby asked for a new assessor and passed a retrieval placement. Lightfoot said she found Letby to be a cold sort of person who lacked warmth.

She said that at the time Letby had trouble when it came to memorising dosages and wasn't quite ready to be a nurse. Nicola Lightfoot said that Letby was not very good interacting with children and patient relatives and had a glum 'expressionless look' which made her come across as blank and aloof. In echo of what Melanie Taylor had said, Lightfoot also said Letby seemed inappropriately excited and desperate to tell people when a baby died. It appears that Letby and Nicola Lightfoot did not get on very well. Neither had anything good to say about the other.

The Thirwall Inquiry, predictably, has not been welcomed very much by Letby's supporters (by supporters I mean the people online who insist she is innocent). Supporters of Letby have complained about 'character assassination' from witnesses and even grumbled about the fact that Letby's parents were not allowed to attend. Letby's barrister Mark McDonald also complained to the media that he had been banned from the inquiry. Mr McDonald was annoyed that one of the legal representatives of the family seemed to ascribe crimes to Letby that she was not convicted of at her trial. McDonald also argued that, in his view, Letby had a right (through him) to challenge the inquiry evidence that dislodgement of breathing tubes had gone up by 40% when Letby was working in Liverpool. His general argument was that the inquiry was one-sided and gave Letby no voice. But then what did he expect? This wasn't an appeal or a retrial. It was an inquiry into how a convicted serial killer was able to go unchecked in a hospital.

The inquiry wasn't interested in questioning Letby's guilt because as far as they were concerned a jury had already decided that issue. That wasn't the remit of the inquiry. So this was a frustrating spectacle for supporters of Letby. This inquiry has not gone terribly well for Lucy Letby. It hasn't done much to bolster her claims of innocence. In fact, fresh revelations from the inquiry even made the New Yorker edit parts of their piece questioning Letby's conviction. The inquiry has made no discernible difference though to the online campaigners convinced that Lucy Letby is innocent. They'll simply call it a whitewash. Mark McDonald called the growing background chatter from those convinced Letby is innocent the 'elephant in the room'. The inquiry, aside from some comments at the start, was doing its level best to ignore this elephant.

The inquiry heard that two years before the events which eventually got Letby convicted, she had given a baby ten times the prescribed amount of morphine. Thankfully, the mistake was noticed and the baby was fine in the end. As a result of this, Letby was given extra training and not allowed to administer drugs for a time. The inquiry heard that Letby was not very happy about being prevented from administering drugs to patients. There was also another incident where Letby gave antibiotics to a baby which had not been prescribed antibiotics. In a hospital review, Letby had said it was an unavoidable error. Yvonne Farmer, who was practice development nurse at the time, told the inquiry it was not an unavoidable error and said she had no idea why Letby was giving unprescribed drugs to a baby.

Yvonne Griffiths, who was deputy ward manager of the neonatal unit, said in her inquiry evidence that the whispers against Letby by doctors felt like a 'witch hunt' at the time and made the nursing staff close ranks around Letby. They felt as if the finger of suspicion was being pointed at the nurses as a whole. Around this time an edition of Panorama was devoted to the Lucy Letby case. The special noted the band of online sceptics and professional medical experts who either believe Letby is innocent or find that the evidence used to convict her was not conclusive. The edition of Panorama revealed that when Letby was training in Liverpool a third of all emergencies happened on her shift. Panorama also revealed that another infant (not mentioned at the trial) was allegedly poisoned with insulin at Chester while Letby was working there. Panorama stated that the infant got ill soon after Letby started her shift but recovered after her shift ended.

Eirian Powell, who was the manager of the hospital's neonatal unit (and got a lot of retrospective criticism), was a much anticipated witness at the Thirwall Inquiry. Eirian Powell's staunch support for Letby was often cited as consultants as a reason for the hospital dithering for so long over whether to bring in the police. Some of the other nurses said that Letby was a particular favourite of Eirian Powell. In her evidence, Eirian Powell described Lucy Letby as an excellent nurse. Powell said all the nursing staff were sceptical about the allegations against Letby and didn't believe them. They did though study the duty logs and find Letby was a common denominator. Eirian Powell said she didn't really take this as proof of guilt because Letby did a lot of extra shifts so was at the hospital all the time. Eirian Powell denied that Letby (who she called 'Lucy' at the inquiry) was one of her favourites (teacher's pet if you will). Eirian Powell said she was never presented with any evidence that Letby had done any of these things and so wouldn't do anything differently if she could go back. She did say though that in hindsight the police should have been called sooner.

Karen Rees, who was head of nursing at the time Letby worked at the hospital in Chester, had been heavily criticised in the wake of the trial for refusing to take any action when concerns about Letby were expressed by some of the doctors. At the Thirwall Inquiry, Rees was given a chance to defend herself. She targeted Dr Stephen Brearey in particular in her inquiry evidence. "I said: Look, you need to share with me why you've got these concerns, and why, and how do you think she's purposefully harming babies?" she told the inquiry. "His answer to me, and I remember it clearly, because he said: 'I've got a gut feeling and I've got a drawer of doom' and he pointed to a drawer in his desk. So I said to him will you share the contents of that drawer, of which he refused. He just said she needs to be moved off the neonatal unit. I am aware that she's on this weekend. So I said to him: I can't remove a nurse from a clinical practice just because you've got a feeling and a drawer of doom which you will not share with me. So I wasn't getting anywhere with him." Karen Rees said she was annoyed when Dr Brearey later called her at home. "I felt like I was being bullied and intimidated, I didn't find it a very professional conversation. Why tell me he's got a drawer of doom and not share the contents with me?"

Karen Rees told the inquiry that she wondered at first if there was some personal issue between Letby and Dr Brearey. There was even a rumour that they'd had an affair or maybe he had made a pass at Letby and been rebuffed. None of this was true of course but it was briefly pondered as a possible theory. Karen Rees conceded that she had got too 'close' to Letby and this might have clouded her judgement. The inquiry heard that even several months after the police were contacted, Rees was still sending Letby supportive texts. Karen Rees said Letby was devastated when she was moved to a clerical job. "She kept crying, asking, "Why are they doing this to me, I've done nothing wrong, I'm not going to let them run me out of a job I love.' I suppose months of that, her being distressed. I remember looking at her and thinking, this is dreadful." Under questioning, Rees agreed that concerns from consultants should in hindsight have prompted the immediate removal of Lucy Letby from her duties. Rees also agreed that the safety of the patients should have superseded the complaints of Letby and her parents over the way she was being treated. Karen Rees said she was greatly relieved when the police were called in because the internal hospital investigations were getting nowhere and going around in circles.

Anne Murphy, the lead nurse for children's services at the time Letby worked in the hospital, echoed the evidence of other nursing staff by saying that the evidence against Letby was vague. "I don't think we felt as nurses that we could accuse her of doing some harm without actual evidence and the fact that the babies appeared to die of, you know, varying conditions and there was nothing at post-mortem to say that there was anything different at that time, I don't think we felt that it was fair that a nurse should be accused. If that had been a member of the medical staff I would have felt the same thing you know, what proof did we have that there was any wrongdoing? At that stage, it was generally thought that everything had to be reviewed - not just the fact that there was a nurse they felt was potentially involved [but] all the other elements - the care practices, the standards that were there, infection control issues. There still wasn't any evidence that she had done any wrong."

Annemarie Lawrence, a former midwife who worked in an adjoining office to Lucy Letby when Letby was moved to a desk job in the complaints department, said that Letby may have accessed medical files in her office job because she seemed to know exactly what was happening on the wards and units. "I was coming into work one morning and as I came up the stairs Lucy came out of her office on the corridor to greet me and she was very distressed. She almost jumped down my throat really and said 'there's been a collapse and a baby has been transferred out, does that mean somebody else

is going to be under investigation and I can go back to work?'
She bombarded me with a lot of questions and I didn't know
what she was talking about because I wasn't aware of a
collapse .. but she knew this information and it had not
reached me. Lucy had access to information which she
shouldn't have and I wondered whether there was someone
on the neonatal unit who is feeding her information but it
concerns me that she knows something clinically that I don't
know as the risk lead."

Annemarie Lawrence said she became suspicious of Letby
when she studied the duty rota in relation to infant
emergencies and saw that Letby was the nurse on shift the
most when these things happened. Lawrence said that she
was told by senior staff to be very 'careful' about allegations
without evidence and told a duty rota link was not sufficient
evidence in and of itself. "I was working alongside somebody
who initially I had thought had done some terrible, terrible
crimes but I felt ashamed for raising them. And then I spent
some time thinking if I had just raised them a little bit louder
then potentially I could have prevented the deaths of two of
those babies, and I didn't. And then I had to work alongside
her and listen to conversations that perhaps she might have
been innocent, and it was really difficult." The Countess of
Chester Hospital's former deputy director of nursing Sian
Williams told the inquiry that she was asked to compose a
duty rota which showed who was working when the deaths
and emergencies occurred. Ms Williams said she was
'spooked' to see that emergencies were 80% more likely to
happen when Letby was on duty.

Sian Williams, though not specifying which child, said she
became suspicious of Letby when she noticed a certain infant
seemed to be poorly when Letby was on duty but recover
when she wasn't there. Ms Williams apologised to parents for

being part of a hospital cover up which concealed information from them. She said she had urged calling the police because she'd been in a hospital many years ago where foul play was suspected and the police were called. Ms Williams said she knew from experience that when it came to this sort of thing the police didn't like hospitals investigating themselves. Around this time, the pro-Letby camp were encouraged by an article in the Telegraph by Sarah Knapton. Knapton is the paper's 'science editor' and would appear to be sceptical about the convictions if her articles are anything to go by. The latest article stated that Dr Jane Hawdon, a consultant neonatologist at the Royal Free Hospital in London, had reviewed the deaths at the Countess of Chester Hospital in 2016. This was not news because most people following the case already knew that.

Knapton's big exclusive was that this report had been leaked to the Telegraph and it stated that sub-optimal care was responsible for most of the deaths and many of them could be medically explained. On the face of it this was a very big deal. The article was basically saying that Dr Hawdon believed most of the deaths were down to natural causes - including the ones Letby was convicted of. This would mean that Dr Hawdon's secret report suggested the case against Letby wasn't safe. Dr Hawdon's mythical report (confusingly, there were three reports by Hawdon it seems) had been a regular piece of evidence for the Private Eye columns which seemed to mock the guilty verdict (and Dr Evans in particular). Dr Hawdon's appearance at the Thirwell Inquiry was not good news for either Knapton or Private Eye. Hawdon complained that she wasn't given much information by the hospital for her report and it was 'superficial' - taking only a few days to write. She had no idea there were suspicions of foul play. Dr Hawdon said that with what she now knows she doesn't believe the deaths were a result of poor care or could be explained by natural causes.

The Telegraph exclusive was therefore debunked just 24 hours after it had been published. After brushing themselves down and moving on, the Telegraph swiftly turned to Dr Jo McPartland, a pathologist at Alder Hey hospital who carried out the post-mortem examination on Child D. Letby was prosecuted for air embolism with this infant but Dr McPartland seemed dubious about that theory and told the inquiry the baby had pneumonia (which was already known) and wasn't well. "Not only was there pneumonia," said Dr McPartland, "there were hyaline membranes which indicated acute lung injury which you don't normally see, so that did lead me to believe that there was more extensive lung injury from the pneumonia than you might expect, so that could explain then why the child didn't behave as the clinicians might have expected." Dr McPartland said she hadn't been told there was suspicion of foul play. She said that had she known about the allegations she would have asked for a forensic pathologist to carry out the post-mortem.

For those who believe Letby is innocent, Dr McPartland's evidence was of particular interest because she offered something of an alternative take on Child D to that of the prosecution at Letby's trial. This is what was lacking in Letby's defence at the trial. Even so, Dr McPartland conceded that a forensic post-mortem would have been more thorough and could not say with absolute certainty if the infant died of pneumonia because she would need to review slides which the police took away as evidence. Letby supporters latched onto the evidence by Dr McPartland as if it had blown a hole in the entire prosecution case. But it really hadn't. Some of those who believe Letby is guilty saw the evidence by Dr Hawdon as the final nail in the coffin of those who maintain she is innocent. But a few more nails might be needed yet.

The 13th of November saw the appearance of Dr Ravi Jayaram at the inquiry. Dr Jayaram began by offering an apology to the parents involved the case that he didn't act sooner and go straight to the police. "It's been said to me in many different fora, why didn't you just pick up the phone to the police, or why didn't you raise it with somebody else, or why didn't you do anything at all?" Jayaram told the inquiry. "I lie awake thinking about this, there's a fear because it is such a seemingly outlandish, and unlikely, thing – that someone is causing deliberate harm. It's the fear of not being believed, it's the fear of ridicule, it's the fear or accusations of bullying. I should have been braver, I should have more courage." Dr Jayaram refuted any claims that he was mistaken about the incident where he walked in on Letby with Child K and found the infant deteriorating and a breathing tube dislodged. "It's been suggested to me that I just made that up, which is, you know, I refute, it's nonsense. There's no reason I would."

Dr Jayaram said he first began to have suspicions about Letby after the case of Child I. It was at this point, said Jarayam, that consultants began to have 'conversations in corridors' about how Letby always seemed to be present at these emergencies. There wasn't much in Dr Jayaram's evidence that we hadn't already heard from the trial and Child K retrial. He was critical of the hospital management but also conceded he should have taken more direct action himself if he suspected deliberate harm from a member of staff. Dr Jayaram said he couldn't be sure if a chest drain valve had been accidentally knocked in the case of Child I. He also said he was annoyed when he had to apologise to Lucy Letby and Letby had said she was coming back whether he liked it or not. In the great wild west court of the internet, Dr Jayaram was now second only to Dr Evans when it came to the gallery of villains for Letby supporters. He was a 'liar' and 'coward' according to some of the angry daily reviews coming from this quarter.

The Letby circus rolled on, nearly everyone becoming more entrenched than ever.

In his final comments, Dr Jayaram made an explicit reference to the 'Letby is Innocent' movement as he again apologised to the parents. "I know that my words will never ever help to ease the grief that you feel and I also want to reach out to you and I'm sorry that you are having to go through the external noise that's out there of people taking another view on everything that's happened and I appreciate how painful that must be for you and how insensitive it is of the people who are trying to suggest that other things happened." Another of the 'gang of four', Dr Stephen Brearey, also gave evidence to the Thirwall Inquiry. Dr Brearey told the inquiry that in his view Letby didn't suddenly become a serial killer in 2015. He believed she probably started harming infants before this period. In reference to the 'drawer of doom' that Karen Rees said he wouldn't show her, Dr Brearey said, "The way that phrase [drawer of doom] has been used by Karen Rees, and was used by others in the following year or so, was belittling the concerns we had. They felt there was no evidence and the consultants were acting inappropriately."

Asked why he did not make a connection between deteriorations in infants and the possibility of foul play sooner, Dr Brearey told the inquiry, "I accept it wasn't in my mind and it's obviously something I have reflected upon and it should have been. It probably comes down to the workload I had at the time in doing this. Most of the reviews were done out of hours. Dealing with mortality on their own was quite a considerable workload along with my other duties. On reflection I do feel there was a lot of clues and incidents, in terms of the morbidity side of things, that would have brought us to the conclusion earlier that something was wrong." Dr Brearey said the determination of the hospital management to stifle any discussion about Lucy Letby made him feel like he was working in North Korea. Brearey said it was hard to imagine anything more incompetent in NHS history than the management clearing Letby to go back to work and telling the consultants to apologise to her.

There was an odd new development when the inquiry asked Dr Brearey about his past suggestions that some of the hospital bosses were freemasons and looking after one another (presumably in some sort of masonic conspiracy). Brearey confirmed that people did have these sorts of impressions. Apropos of nothing, Stephen Cross, who was solicitor for the Countess of Chester Hospital NHS Foundation Trust, is a director of the Chester Freemasons. There are rumours that Lucy Letby's dad is a mason - which might explain why he seemed to be so involved and so influential when there were grievances against his daughter at the hospital. These are purely rumours though and not relevant anyway to the broader question of Letby's guilt. The inquiry also heard that a team from the Care Quality Commission (CQC) watchdog undertook a routine inspection of the Countess of Chester Hospital over four days in February 2016 but were not told about the spike in deaths at the hospital. Had they been told about this they would have investigated and asked questions. The hospital bosses clearly didn't want this to happen at that time.

THE SECOND APPEAL

The Thirwall Inquiry span on with conclusions to be drawn near the end of 2025. Evidence will continue to be heard beyond 2024. As far as the wider debate over Letby's guilt goes, the inquiry has little relevance to that. The only way that it would be relevant to Letby's supporters is if new and damning evidence about care failings in the hospital came to light. Even that though wouldn't instantly spring Letby from prison. Her legal team are going to have to come up with evidence so compelling it proves beyond doubt Letby couldn't have harmed those infants deliberately. Letby's new barrister Mark McDonald seems to be confident he can do that but it won't be easy. In the quest to win the right to appeal against her conviction for the attempted murder of Child K, Letby's court barrister Ben Myers KC argued that the retrial shouldn't have gone ahead because media coverage now made it impossible for Lucy Letby to get a fair hearing.

Myers was basically calling this abuse of process. There is an abuse of process where the prosecutor can be said to have manipulated or misused the rules of procedure or where inordinate delay has prejudiced the defendant to a situation where a fair trial is no longer possible. The London Court of Appeal hearing was presided over by Lord Justice William Davis, sitting with Lord Justice Jeremy Baker and Mrs Justice McGowan. The argument of Ben Myers was that the negative media coverage of Lucy Letby since her original convictions now made it impossible for her to get a fair hearing in any retrial. On the face of it this was a strange argument because Letby had been convicted of murdering infants. The fact that she got some negative press as a result of this was not exactly a big surprise or unreasonable. Ted Bundy had more than one trial but no one argued the second one was unfair because he got some bad press notices after the first one. Serial killers tend not to be beloved in the media.

As evidence, Mr Myers cited a number of examples. These included Rishi Sunak, in his capacity as prime minister, criticising Lucy Letby for not turning up to her sentencing. Myers also cited a Loose Women episode centred around Letby being evil. Mr Myers also complained that the police had been 'prejudiced' in their comments about Letby after she was found guilty. The argument of Myers in this specific point was that the police knew full well there might be retrials so should have kept quiet. Mr Myers also complained about Letby being compared to Rosemary West and Myra Hindley in the newspapers. Mr Myers further complained that Dr Jayaram was permitted to do interviews and talk about Letby despite the fact he was plainly going to be the most salient witness in the Child K retrial. The prosecution argued though that Letby's crimes (for which she was convicted by a jury) were so awful that the media reaction was perfectly normal. Mr Myers, while pointing out that Lucy Letby maintained she was innocent, did have to acknowledge that what she had been convicted of was appalling and constituted the most heinous crimes.

Some of the examples cited by Ben Myers were a bit ridiculous. One was a Mirror article titled Inside Lucy Letby's £200k Beige Home. The article began in this fashion - 'The three-bedroom, semi-detached property is located on Westbourne Road, Chester, just a five-minute drive from the Countess of Chester Hospital, where she carried out her campaign of terror...' A (rather dull) article with descriptions of Letby's interior décor didn't feel outrageously impartial or relevant. The fact that Letby had purchased a house in 2016 did though partly explain why she did so many extra shifts in the hospital. In his rebuttal for the prosecution, Nick Johnson KC pointed out that Ben Myers had agreed that Letby's convictions could be mentioned at the retrial. He also pointed out that when the retrial for the Child K case was announced, reporting restrictions were put in place.

Mr Johnson did something very clever in his rebuttal. He turned the pro-Letby lobby to his advantage and used it as ammunition against Mr Myers. Nick Johnson, countering the defence argument that the media had been prejudiced against Letby, cited the New Yorker article about the case. The article in the New Yorker seemed to suggest that Letby was innocent and some bungling kangaroo court in England had wrongfully imprisoned this modern day Florence Nightingale. "If ever this court wants evidence that publicity had no effect on this jury, this is it," said Mr Johnson. "Because this was very pro-Letby, anti-prosecution material circulating with significant traction on the internet in the weeks and days before the trial. In that context, one remembers the old epithet that today's front page is tomorrow's fish and chip wrappers. The application appears to rely on the huge volume of publicity as being of itself sufficient grounds on which to base an application to stay the indictment. It also leans heavily on the proposition that it is wrong for a witness to speak to the news media and that fact in itself taints the prosecution to the extent that it should be stayed. This is a misguided approach."

Mr Johnson also mentioned the Conservative member of parliament David Davies (who has since said on television that he is '90%' certain Letby is innocent) using his parliamentary privilege to talk about the New Yorker article despite reporting restrictions. Mr Johnson used these things to point out that the coverage of Letby went both ways. It wasn't all negative. Mr Johnson also said that articles about Letby peaked in the aftermath of the convictions and then petered out. He disputed the idea that the media talked about nothing but Lucy Letby. Mr Johnson did concede that the police these days have a tendency to make emotional statements to the media after big cases have concluded with a trial verdict. Mr Johnson said this was something the police never used to do in the old days. As this went on, Lucy Letby followed proceedings via a video link from HMP Bronzefield. Letby looked tired and bored and seemed to suppress several yawns. One got the impression that Letby didn't have much hope of this right to appeal bid going in her favour. If that was the case she turned out to be right.

The basis of the appeal was that the judge should have stopped the retrial on the grounds that it was impossible for Letby, now a notorious Beverly Allitt type serial killer in the eyes of the law and much of the media, to get a fair hearing. The Court of Appeal verdict began by stating it was only interested in whether the judge (Mr Justice Goss) was wrong to go ahead with the retrial of Child K. That was the sole remit. Questions arising from evidence in the first trial and indeed questions about Letby's convictions were not of interest to the Court of Appeal. In his reasoning for going ahead with the retrial, Mr Justice Goss had said, "I am satisfied that any prejudice to the defendant from the publicity in the media is not such as to preclude the defendant from having a fair trial. The evidence of her convictions will be in evidence before the jury. It will be subject to the necessary directions to the jury as to the use to which they may and may not put this evidence; they will also receive a direction as to the importance of reaching their verdict on, and only on the evidence placed before them and nothing else. Experience has shown that juries can be relied upon faithfully to follow such directions. The media coverage will, in any event, have been diluted by the 'fade factor' since the verdicts in the original trial were reported."

'The judge identified that to stay a criminal trial because it would offend the integrity of the justice system always will be the remedy of last resort,' concluded the Court of Appeal. 'It is an exceptional step to take. It was not justified by the circumstances in this case. The judge was entirely correct to find that it would not be unfair to try Lucy Letby for the single offence of attempted murder. It follows that we refuse her application for leave to appeal against conviction. We repeat what we said earlier. This application related to a narrow legal issue. Nothing we have said can contribute to any debate about the wider case against Lucy Letby.' The Court of appeal verdict also dismissed the complaints of Mr Myers about the police speaking to the media after the original trial with 'hostile' comments about Lucy Letby. The Court of appeal ruled that it was frankly ridiculous to complain about a woman convicted of murdering babies being spoken of in less than flattering terms by the police officers who had built the case against her. What did Mr Myers expect the police to say? That she was a lovely person and probably innocent?

The Court of Appeal verdict dismissed the argument by Letby's barrister that Dr Jayaram had prejudiced the retrial by speaking to the media after Letby's original convictions. 'Following Letby's convictions he had been interviewed by a variety of outlets and had commented on social media about the case. The schedule of material relating specifically to him indicates that he ceased to comment once it was known that there was to be a re-trial in relation to the count with which he was particularly concerned. But the submission is that his public statements prior to that were "extraordinary" given his position as a witness. We do not agree with that proposition. We have reviewed the material relating to Dr Jayaram with care. We could not identify any matter relating to Letby which significantly departed from the evidence he gave in the two trials. He made comments about the extent to which those with overall charge of the neo-natal unit bore responsibility for what had occurred. This could not have prejudiced the case against Letby.'

Lucy Letby displayed no emotion at the news her right to appeal bid had been refused. By the look of her resigned, disinterested expression, she hadn't expected anything else. Lord Justice Davis said while Letby's original convictions 'undoubtedly led to an unusually large amount of publicity and online debate,' it was because the case was 'extraordinary'. Simply because the extent of the publicity was much greater than would normally be the case of itself did not generate prejudice. For a neo-natal nurse to murder seven babies in her care was a startling fact, even if no police officer or other commentator had said anything about Letby being comparable to other notorious murderers or used extreme adjectives to describe her, the mere fact of her offending would have created that effect.'

While it was possible to understand where Ben Myers was coming from in arguing that it was impossible for Letby to have a retrial where the jury had no preconceived opinions on her it was hard to see how the complaint could have been witheld. Mr Myers was basically saying that criminals shouldn't face retrials due to bad publicity from their crimes! Lucy Letby didn't expect much from this appeal bid so the verdict was probably not a great surprise or crushing blow to her. Her only hope now was that her new barrister could somehow pull a rabbit out of a hat with some new evidence. Mark McDonald was certainly doing a lot of interviews in his new capacity as Letby's barrister. He seemed to be on a PR campaign designed to keep her case in the public eye. While he hadn't come up with much that was new besides regurgitating arguments Letby's supporters had said a million times online already, his calm, laid-back and friendly persona was at least a positive.

THE CIRCUS

All through this case, especially since the trial, there have been those who either flat out don't believe Letby is guilty or those who were not impressed by the prosecution evidence at the trial and so remain ambiguous. Soon this all began to spiral until it became a loud background noise. Suddenly, people on Twitter and forums who were not even at the trial and had no medical qualifications were now all medical experts who knew much more about this case than real doctors and professors who actually testified at the trial. The Countess of Chester Hospital was depicted as being like something out of The Flintstones. It was rife with bacteria, the sinks overflowed, there were hardly any staff, everyone was incompetent and had no idea what they were doing. The staff were not merely incompetent. Some of them were evil and decided to frame an innocent salsa dancing young nurse for multiple murders in order to cover up care failings at the hospital. Dr Dewi Evans, the chief prosecution witness, was a 'nonce' and a 'liar' according to some of the more ill disciplined and hysterical of Letby's supporters. Crazy blog posts have compared Lucy Letby to witches burned at the stake in the sixteenth century. How did we end up in this situation?

A lot of people on Mumsnet think Letby is innocent. The celebrity judge Rob Rinder has expressed his doubts about the trial. There were articles in the New Yorker (one might suggest the New Yorker could spend a bit more time investigating all the potential miscarriages of justice in the United States before turning their attention to Lucy Letby across the Atlantic) and The Guardian and also a Channel 5 documentary which all cast some doubt on the safety of the conviction. The Telegraph's science editor, as we mentioned, seems to be sympathetic to the view that the conviction wasn't safe. Politicians like David Davis (the bungling Brexit Secretary described as 'thick as mince' by Dominic Cummings) and self-appointed know-it-all's like the Daily Mail columnist Peter Hitchens expressed concern over the safety of the conviction. John Sweeney took a brief break from

Russia's invasion of Ukraine to arrange his own crowdfunded podcast tuppence on why Lucy Letby was innocent. A Hospital Full of S*** was the title of his opening salvo - with much weight (too much you might venture) given to the bewildered plumber who gave evidence at Letby's trial.

Nadine Dorries, the former Health Secretary, was also critical of Letby's trial in her newspaper column. "It appears to me a pattern that might arise in any hospital ward that experienced a cluster of deaths. For example, a report last year found that 201 new-borns may have died at the Shrewsbury and Telford Hospital NHS Trust due to a lack of appropriate care. If a similar graph were drawn there, might it show that one nurse was consistently present at several of the deaths? And would that necessarily be enough to put this nurse in prison for the rest of her life?"

Steve Phelps, a television producer who worked on Dispatches and Rough Justice, said the Letby case has "all the characteristics of an egregious miscarriage of justice" and argued that the hospital in Chester wasn't equipped to deal with new infants. David Livermore, a professor of medical microbiology at the University of East Anglia, believes that infection was the most likely cause of the spike in infant deaths at the hospital where Letby worked. 'Letby's 'crime' was to be fool enough to remain in a badly-run and contaminated unit working far beyond its competency,' wrote Livermore. 'Even less wise, she accepted every shift she could because she was saving to buy a house.'

Doctors, scientists, statisticians, and conspiracy theorists began to join the chorus. It may or may not come as a surprise to know that David Icke believes Letby is innocent. David Icke is best known for his claim that the shadowy elites who run the world are in reality blood drinking alien reptiles from another dimension. Icke believes the British Royal Family are shapeshifting reptile aliens who take part in human sacrifice and Satanic blood drinking rituals. David Icke also says the moon is hollow and a giant signals station for alien mind control signals that come from Saturn. Icke claims the Illuminati like to hunt humans for sport in a 'Most Dangerous Game' type of scenario. According to Icke, figures like Bill Clinton and the Bush family hunt mind-controlled slaves through a forest with guns and hunting dogs. Icke has also suggested that cancer is curable with treatments of sodium bicarbonate - which gives you a fair idea of his medical credentials. In 1991, Icke predicted that Cuba, Greece, the Isle of Arran, the cliffs of Kent, and Teeside would be submerged by a great earthquake. He also predicted that New Zealand would vanish in an ecological disaster. 'Mr Icke has since stated that at the time he made these predictions he knew they were crazy,' wrote the late paranormal debunker James Randi. 'I have no disagreement with that evaluation.'

In 2020, David Icke was removed from social media platforms for comments he made about the coronavirus. These were deemed misleading and potentially dangerous. What exactly did David Icke say about the coronavirus? Icke said that he and his son had the coronavirus before it was well known and that it was no worse than a bout of the flu. He claimed its effects had been grossly exaggerated. David Icke has said there are many doctors and medical experts who support this view but that they are not allowed on the mainstream media so you never hear them speak. Icke has gone so far as to suggest that the virus doesn't actually exist and that most modern medical complaints are due to 5G sucking oxygen out of the air. Icke has suggested that populations were being locked in their homes so that they couldn't protest against 5G. Icke also said that covid vaccines were laced with nanotechnology to control us. So, presumably, if you had a covid jab, according to David Icke you are going to end up like that woman in Superman III who got turned into a robot. David Icke has also been banned from some countries for alleged antisemitism.

Among the latest to join the Lucy Letby is Innocent bandwagon is Dan Wootton - a former breakfast television showbusiness fluff reporter and GB news presenter. Mr Wootton's evidence for Letby being innocent includes (much like Mr Sweeney) 'sewage in the sinks' (how sewage manage to poison babies with insulin and over-feed them with milk so far remains unexplained - was this sewage sentient and capable of morphing into different shapes?) and the fact that (boo!) the Health Secretary West Streeting MP thinks Letby is guilty. If a Labour minister and the MSM (mainstream media) think Letby is guilty then that's more than enough for Wootton to hitch his wagon to the contrarian camp. Another journalist who has said the Letby conviction was unsafe is Owen Jones. Owen Jones is a political commentator with his own column in The Guardian. Even if you avoid The Guardian there is no escape from Jones as he's constantly on television acting as if he's the world's leading expert on everything. Despite the fact that he went to Oxford University and has never done a day's work in his life, Jones thinks of himself as a spokesperson for the working-class.

As you can see then, we have an eclectic stew of people in the media and beyond who have piped up about the Letby case. David Davis said the late billionaire Mike Lynch, who tragically died in a yachting accident, had doubts about the Letby conviction and planning to set up an 'Innocence Project' to help. "Mike was a world-class expert on probability theory," said Davis, "and saw straight through the statistical weaknesses that underpinned the Letby prosecution." But statistics didn't underpin the Letby prosecution did they? It was medical evidence wasn't it? You can't try and bend every piece of evidence or crime case into a debate about statistics. In his own detective work on the case, Peter Hitchens cited Science on Trial as an especially interesting and valuable source of information when it came to the Lucy Letby affair. He was not the only prominent supporter or sceptic to plug Science on Trial as the capital city of information when it came to debunking the convictions against Letby.

Science on Trial was set up by a woman named Sarrita Adams. As far as the Letby lobby goes, you could say that Sarrita Adams was the first out of the gate. Sarrita Adams was billed as a British born California-based scientific consultant for biotech start-ups. She said she had a PhD from Cambridge University. The PhD was in Biochemistry with focus on 'rare diseases'. Adams declared that the conviction of Lucy Letby was a massive miscarriage of justice and promised to use science to prove this. For a time, Sarrita Adams (through Science on Trial and the website rexvlucyletby2023.com) was more or less the leader of the Letby is Innocent collective. Her posts and articles on Letby's innocence were enthusiastically reposted by them and they acted as if she was some lofty genius who knew more about this case than anyone. The most vocal of Letby's online supporters were naturally delighted to have this Cambridge University educated expert on rare diseases on their team. Dr Adams, as she liked to be billed, was now on the case. It was surely only a matter of time before Lucy Letby - through the power of science, reason, and the mighty intellect of Sarrita Adams - was cleared and released.

Sarrita Adams used her great 'expertise' to challenge the doctors who gave evidence at the trial. She was confident that she knew a lot more about medicine and rare diseases than these humble doctors and professors. Science on Trial offered alternative explanations for the deaths at the Chester neonatal unit and pointed out all the things the doctors had allegedly missed. Adams was probably the original pedlar of the infection theory. The idea that the hospital had a bug outbreak. It can't be a coincidence that the infection theory was then latched onto by some of Letby's loudest online supporters. Sarrita Adams pompously announced online that she spent her days 'cleaning up the mess' of doctors who 'routinely' miss or misdiagnose the expert evidence on rare diseases she supplies. Adams said the claims against Letby were 'provably' wrong and that doctors she knew in the United States were baffled by how these stupid British doctors were so dim that they missed all this scientific and medical evidence which proved that Letby was innocent. Adams pointedly never named any of these clever American doctors who thought the doctors involved in the Letby case were idiots.

Adams said that the doctors in Chester failed to spot the existing medical conditions of the infants. They also got the insulin readings wrong. Adams also pointed out that we just had a world wide pandemic where some people died. What this last point had to do with the price of fish remains a mystery. Some of the more prominent supporters of Letby gave money to Sarrita Adams. Science on Trial was a profit organisation and claimed to be fundraising to collect cash for Lucy Letby's appeal. This made no sense because Letby's right to appeal wouldn't cost her any money. It would be free through legal aid. Where was all the money raised by Sarrita Adams going? Adams also appealed to fundraisers to help them set up other campaigns to challenge the 'poor use of science in the criminal justice system'. Science on Trial, as a website, soon began to raise a few red flags. The scientific and medical facts for one thing often seemed, well, like science jargon gobbledygook. Sarrita Adams also sounded a bit angry in her posts sometimes. Slightly unhinged you would say for a

Cambridge educated genius who knew more about medicine than all the doctors in Chester put together.

So, predictably, some began to suspect that Sarrita Adams was a grifter. A charlatan who was using the Letby case to make money from donations. A woman named Amy Gulley was dubious about the credentials of Sarrita Adams and so set up a subreddit called r/scienceontrial to discuss Adams and her website. In response, Sarrita Adams took out a restraining order which banned Gulley from talking about her online or 'impersonating' her by using the Science on Trial name. Gulley, who lived in another state, was bemused by this legal action. She hired a legal team who argued that the restraining order was in violation of freedom of speech. The restraining order was quashed in the end but not before Gulley's legal team uncovered something very interesting - which was also confirmed by documents in the divorce case of Sarrita Adams. It turned out that the PhD in Biochemistry from Cambridge Univirsity which Adams liked to boast about was fake. She hadn't even got the name of the college right on her bogus certificate.

Sarrita Adams always claimed to have a background in forensic science - which was also false. Adams was a fraud. Sarrita Adams has since deleted all of her social media and the Science on Trial website. One of her last crazy posts (before she sensibly vanished from the net) was as a sock puppet fictious woman writing (for some reason in the style of a 1930s washerwoman from the deep south) about how 'Miss Adams' had miraculously saved her son from a rare disease. And yet, Sarrita Adams and Science on Trial had been frequently cited by people online as evidence that Letby was innocent. Dr Phil Hammond, who writes about the Letby case for Private Eye, is another who appears to have been duped by Sarrita Adams as he once suggested her as someone that Lucy

Letby's defence team could have called on to help. Letby can count herself very lucky this didn't happen.

Rachel Aviv, who wrote the New Yorker article which depicted the Letby case as a gross miscarriage of justice against a sweet poor young woman, consulted Sarrita Adams as an 'expert' - which obviously hasn't aged very well. Aviv was in email contact with Sarrita Adams in 2023 and told Adams that she read all the Science on Trial themed posts about the Letby case and wished there were more 'great minds' like hers. This was confirmed in a now deleted Twitter screenshot by Adams. Aviv was also naively unaware that her article could (and would) be used by the prosecution at the appeal to argue against the defence claim that Letby's blanket negative press made retrials unfair. Negative press?, said the prosecution. Have you seen the New Yorker recently? Court documents indicated that Sarrita Adams was mentally incompetent (once breaking into the home of her husband with a knife and spray-painting the wall), guilty of spousal abuse, and unemployed (Adams was said to have a small Etsy store selling berets). Supporters of Lucy Letby, once so seduced by those largely unreadable walls of scientific gibberish endlessly posted on the case, quickly distanced themselves from Sarrita Adams.

Among the online lobby questioning the convictions of Letby, the most sizeable group seems to be statisticians. Statisticians can play a crucial role in criminal cases by providing quantitative analysis that can help to interpret evidence, assess the probability of events, and contribute to expert testimony. In court, statisticians may provide expert testimony regarding the validity of statistical evidence, such as the probability of events occurring under certain conditions, which can influence jury decisions. Statisticians may use Bayesian methods to assess the strength of evidence presented in court, helping to evaluate the probability of a defendant's guilt based on prior knowledge and new evidence. Bayesian methods are a set of statistical techniques that apply Bayes' theorem for updating the probability of a hypothesis as more evidence or information becomes available.

A number of statisticians believe the statistical data in the Letby case was flawed and that the collapses in the neonatal unit as a whole, regardless of whether Letby was there or not, should be looked at to get a more accurate picture. It sometimes feels as if statisticians never believe any criminal is guilty - especially medical killers. One could be forgiven for occasionally having the impression that the statisticians obsessed with the Letby case are desperate to find another Lucia de Berk because statistical evidence was a factor in exonerating Lucia. This is not to disparage statisticians. Their views on the Letby case are deservedly given a regular hearing in the media. The problem is that Letby was not convicted by statistical evidence. Because of past cases where people were wrongly convicted because of faulty statistics, statisticians, when it comes to criminal cases, tend to err on the side of caution. It seems to take a lot to make them think someone is guilty. This is fair enough. There is nothing wrong with demanding more certainty in serious cases.

The prosecution in the Letby did not use statistical data as its main evidence and the defence seemed largely disinterested in this angle too. Ben Myers could have easily put a statistician in the witness box if he'd wanted to but he chose not do this. Dr Dewi Evans, the chief prosecution witness, has indicated he is rather puzzled by statisticians attacking him because in his view statistical data was irrelevant to the convictions. Statisticians have pointed out that just because Letby did a lot of shifts this doesn't automatically mean she was guilty. This is true. It is also true that there have been cases in the past where a nurse was falsely accused of harming patients on the basis of flawed statistical evidence. The Journal of Investigative Psychology Journal of Investigative Psychology and Offender Profiling, in a study of medical killers, wrote that 'attendance data should be treated with caution as evidence in the investigation and prosecution. A spike in the numbers of deaths on the shifts may well be an indicator of wrongdoing. However, this should only be used in combination with other types of evidence.' Those who believe the conviction of Lucy Letby is safe would argue that there were plenty of other 'types' of evidence and statistics were not the major component of the prosecution.

The more vocal supporters of Lucy Letby sometimes get very annoyed if anyone suggests Lucy Letby is guilty and the conviction was sound. They'll say it was a witch-hunt or a cover-up. The prosecution's chief medical witness was incompetent. The insulin readings were wrong. The hospital was a disaster zone. The staffing levels were inadequate. Doctors didn't do enough rounds. Doctors were inexperienced. The water in the unit was contaminated. There were not enough thorough post-mortems. And so on. The only possibility some of them won't consider is that Letby might be guilty. While it is perfectly valid to have doubts about the convictions some believe the cynical contrarian spirit of our age has played a part in this. Are we so distrustful of authority and our institutions that a lengthy criminal investigation and court case is no longer deemed valid but something to be ignored rather than respected? When it comes to newspapers and websites, some wonder if questioning the Lucy Letby verdict has become a grift. Has it become easy clickbait for these newspapers and websites? An innocent woman being put in prison for murdering infants is a much bigger story than a guilty woman being put in prison for murdering infants. You get longevity with the former. You can keep running stories about how she might be innocent forever.

Among the group that make up the sceptics you have the inevitable flock of Tesco Value detectives and pretend medical/scientific experts online who insist Letby is innocent, a lovely sweet person, and act as if they know her personally. Their Twitter feed will be full of smiling pictures of Letby, glass of wine in hand, in happier days and they'll inquire on forums if anyone knows how they can write to 'Lucy' in prison. This group is sometimes called the Letby Truthers. Among the medical professionals who question Letby's convictions you will get a more balanced and considered approach. Their position is usually something along the lines of 'I don't know if she is innocent but I don't think there is evidence to say she is guilty'. Some of these medical professionals have disputed the validity of the prosecution evidence. You could call this group the Agnostics or Doubters. They don't believe there was enough evidence to lock Lucy Letby up for murder. Dr Hall would fall into this category.

Dr Phil Hammond would perhaps also fall broadly into this category (although you'd probably have to ask him to know for sure - he seems to have very grave doubts about the safety of the medical evidence and guilty verdict). Hammond initially assumed Letby must be guilty but changed his mind when he spoke to medical professionals with concerns over the verdict. So, as we noted earlier, you now have this situation of experts versus experts drawing different medical conclusions from the evidence. Those who prosecuted Letby would perhaps say that those who question the verdict don't know the full story. They were not at the trial and did not have access to clinical records. This would not apply to Dr Hall though because he was at the trial and reviewed all the infant cases that Letby was charged with. If there is a main theme among the medical professionals dubious about the Letby convictions it concerns the competence of the hospital in Chester and also doubt over the diagnosis of air embolism by Dr Evans as a main factor.

Some of the Letby supporters would point out hospital care scandals in the past. This is a perfectly valid issue because there have been some awful NHS care failings and the hospital in Chester should be scrutinised as thoroughly as possible. This is ostensibly one of the points of the Thirwall Inquiry but Letby supporters and even agnostics tend to be dismayed by and dismissive of the inquiry because it has no remit to question Letby's guilt. So this whole circus goes around in circles. There are now even two Lucy Letby subreddits - one which accepts she is guilty and another which maintains she is innocent. The two groups exist in parallel universes from one another where a different reality prevails. Give the wrong opinion on Letby in the wrong Reddit group and you will get downvoted or even banned. There are alternate reality versions of Lucy Letby in these groups. One version of Lucy Letby is the most evil British serial killer in recent memory and the other version of Lucy Letby is a kind, caring young woman who has been stitched-up by heartless hospital bigwigs and doctors. Which one is the real Lucy Letby?

Is the guilty verdict more difficult to accept because Lucy Letby was a young blonde-haired white woman who looked like your neighbour or friend? The novelist Joanne Harris tweeted that, in her view, "The Letby case should teach us this: Too many people think 'innocence' looks white, middle-class, traditional, vulnerable, tearful. People who present this way are often unquestioningly believed and supported." And what was the motive? The police could find no reason why Letby would murder infants. Because they were convicted of similar crimes, Letby was sometimes compared to Beverley

Allitt in the media. The same Beverley Allitt who would leave human faeces in the fridge as a prank when she was a student nurse. The same Beverley Allitt who betrays more than a hint of madness in old photographs. Lucy Letby on the other hand had nothing in her past to indicate darkness or mental instability. Letby is vanilla ice cream and ready salted crisps girl next door in her old photographs. Smiling beige Lucy. In psychology, this is sometimes called the halo effect. We have an unconscious bias towards people we perceive to be attractive or 'normal' looking. We assume they must be nice people.

When he was on trial for murder, the evil serial killer Ted Bundy had female groupies in court each day to support him. Many of his friends refused to believe that 'nice Ted' could possibly be guilty. Hybristophilia has reared its head in the Lucy Letby affair too - with Letby the recipient of 'fan mail' in prison. So why the obsession with Lucy Letby? The male nurse Colin Norris was convicted of murdering elderly patients with insulin injections and has been in prison for a long time now. One could argue that the conviction of Colin Norris is more questionable than that of Lucy Letby. Paul Moffitt, the Jury Foreman at the trial of Colin Norris, now believes that Norris is innocent after hearing an endocrinologist, clinical biochemist, and insulin poisoning expert express their own doubts about the guilty verdict in a documentary. Despite all of this you don't see a huge concerted online campaign to get Colin Norris out of prison. There is no reddit group for Norris. What is it about the Lucy Letby case which makes so many people believe she is innocent and determined to campaign for her?

Is it because Colin Norris is a nerdish looking middle-aged gay man who was notoriously choleric in police interviews and in court? Is he less appealing than Lucy Letby? Letby was not choleric or angry in custody and in court. She was quiet and blank. Letby looked bored and disinterested. This could be read as unemotional and cold but to Lucy Letby's defenders she was a poor, frightened women who was probably medicated for depression. We later learned that Letby initially failed final year student nurse placement because she was deemed to be 'cold' with patients and patient relatives. Letby seemed to lack empathy. When there was a death in her unit she often couldn't wait to tell someone as if this was an exciting piece of news which simply had to be shared. Conspiracy theorists (not that all Letby supporters are conspiracy theorists) and contrarians often tend to distrust institutions. Those who support Lucy Letby clearly do not trust the NHS because the whole basis of their argument is that the medical establishment either framed Letby to mask care failings or wrongly concluded she might be a killer.

As for the legal system, after a lengthy months long trial, Lucy Letby was found guilty and sentenced to life in prison. Lucy Letby's defenders believe this verdict was wrong. So they do not have faith in the marathon trial which, in mind numbing detail, examined the case for the defence (admittedly without defence witnesses save for Letby and a plumber) and the prosecution. To her most fervent supporters the trial was a whitewash and kangaroo court. Will this interest in Lucy Letby ever peter out and dampen down? It seems probable that Letby will be less reported in the end so long as she remains in prison but interest in the case will never completely peter out and those who believe she is innocent are unlikely to drift away. The interest in the Letby case was re-activated by the Child K retrial and Thirwall Inquiry but what happens after this remains to be seen. It will presumably be quieter (in that Letby will no longer be a daily feature of news reports) but the doubts some have about the conviction are not going to go away. The enduring fascination with this case resides in the possibility of a twist. Some breakthrough by Letby's barrister which shakes the foundations of the convictions and demands that the case be looked at again.

Purely as a hypothetical exercise, what would happen if there was a retrial? Would the result be any different? Lucy Letby would have some some advantages in a retrial that she didn't enjoy in the original trial. For a start she would have a modest wind behind her from all the people who have cast doubt on the convictions. One would presume her barrister in the retrial would actually call medical experts as witnesses this time - which would help. Dr Hall might finally get his day in court. The defence in a retrial could also inform the jury about details absent from the original trial - like the fact that Letby's so called confession notes were written on the advice of a therapist. A retrial would still be a formidable challenge though for anyone representing Letby because the prosecution would not be appreciably weaker. No one from prosecution side of the trial has changed their mind or said they think Letby might be innocent. Most of them seem to be more convinced than ever.

One of the odd things to come out of the Lucy Letby case is that you'd sometimes be forgiven, reading the arguments of those who think Letby is innocent, if you got the impression that medical serial killers don't exist. Some of the more extreme Letby supporters give one the impression that the idea of a nurse serial killer is preposterous and should be laughed out of court the moment it rears its head. This is plainly absurd. Indulge me for a moment so we can counter this assumption with a few real life cases. Marianne Nölle was born in 1938 in Cologne, North Rhine-Westphalia, Germany. Nölle is another in the long line of medical killers. To the world at large she was a competent and respected nurse but in reality she was killed patients with overdoses of Truxal.

Chlorprothixene, sold under the brand name Truxal, is a sedative and antipsychotic. Overdose symptoms can be confusion, hypotension, and tachycardia. Nölle killed seven patients from 1984 to 1992 but she is believed to have attempted to kill around seventeen patients in all. The oldest victim of Marianne Nölle was 91 years-old. None of the victims were terminally ill. Marianne Nölle would rob the victims after she killed them and take any money or valuables they had with them. Her heartless crimes eventually began to attract suspicion. A grandson of one of her victims started to become suspicious and scrutiny of Marianne Nölle became heightened as a consequence.

With more relatives and also a hospital supervisor becoming suspicious, exhumations took place which established that Nölle's patients had not died of natural causes at all. They had been hastened to their grave by this wicked medical killer. Marianne Nölle was 57 years-old by the time of her trial. She sat silent through most of it and only spoke at the end to insist she was innocent. In 1993 she was sentenced to life in prison. Nölle, in a rare show of emotion, became tearful at this. The judge described Marianne Nölle as a very heartless and manipulative two faced woman. Her patients all loved her but little did they know she was only interested in killing them so that she could take what little money or valuables they might have. Marianne Nölle never confessed to any of her crimes or provided any explanation for why she had killed these patients. The judge at the trial said she had taken it upon herself to play 'master' over life and death. Her guilt was never in question as four cans of Truxal were found in her apartment after she was arrested. The chilling thing about Marianne Nölle is that her patients all trusted her because she seemed so genuine and caring. Little did they know how dangerous she really was.

Timea Faludi was born in Hungary in 1977. She was a nurse at the Gyula Nviro Hospital in Budapest and was convicted of murdering dozens of patients. Faludi joined the staff in 1994 and the deaths occurred during the night shifts she worked. She worked at the hospital for six years without raising any alarms and mostly cared for patients who were terminally ill. Faludi became an experienced nurse who was well liked by her colleagues and seemed very professional and good at her job. This all changed though when a colleague saw Faludi giving patients intravenous injections without a doctor's prescription. Euthanasia is illegal in Hungary and she was arrested. Faludi confessed to killing forty patients when she was arrested but then seemed to retract this confession. The authorities could only find evidence for around ten deaths (a lot of the victims had obviously been cremated) - although it seems to be a fairly agreed fact that she killed a lot more people than that.

Faludi claimed that she killed because she wanted to relieve the suffering of patients but prosecutors begged to differ and believed that, like other medical killers, Faludi had developed a God complex and become intoxicated with the power she had over the life and death of patients. Faludi's crimes were mitigated by the fact that the patients she killed were apparently terminally ill. It is for this reason that she received a fairly light sentence of nine years (and was of course banned from ever becoming a nurse again). Was she a cold blooded killer or pure Angel of Mercy? The case against Faludi would point out that her evidence was full of contradictions because she kept changing it (it seems plausible that her lawyers were the main culprits in this).

There is also the fact that the patients she killed, while they might have been ill, did not give their consent for their lives to be terminated (in many cases they were incapable of this).

Would Faludi have killed if she had been caring for non terminal patients? We may already know the answer to that question because two of her victims were not terminally ill and simply waiting for surgery. The court verdict on Faludi stated that - "She alternately put herself in the place of the doctor or in that of the patient and took decisions instead of them. The term euthanasia can only be used at all if a patient expresses a wish to have his or her life terminated. In Faludi's cases, this did not happen." The court called Faludi a rational intelligent women who was trustworthy on the surface but secretly believed she was God. Faludi, who was 25 at the time of the trial, tends to be known as The Black Angel in Hungary. She was released from prison in 2009 and (understandably) maintains a low profile these days.

Dana Sue Gray was born Dana Sue Armbrust in 1957 in southern California. Dana Sue Gray worked as a nurse and killed three older women in a gated community in 1994. The ferocity of the attacks shocked the police. One victim was left with a knife sticking out of her neck and another was strangled with a telephone cord. The motivation of Dana Sue Gray was money. She was addicted to shopping and had run up debts. Gray was what you might describe as a shopaholic. Having no money to buy things made her feel miserable. Gray seemed fairly normal as a young women. She was fond of skydiving and worked hard at nursing school. Gray also loved golf and would take trips to Hawaii to go golfing. She got married (to Tom Gray) in 1987 and the couple dabbled in several business ventures. The marriage didn't last long though and ended around 1993. Dana Sue Gray worked at Inland Valley Regional Medical Center as a nurse but she was fired for stealing painkillers. The business ventures she had with her former husband had practically bankrupted them by now too so things were looking bleak.

If there was one thing Dana hated more than anything else it was not having any money. She therefore resorted to murder to secure what she desired. The victims of Gray were vulnerable and elderly women who lived in the same Canyon Lake gated community that she did. The first victim was 86 year-old Norma Davis. Norma was found with a knife in her neck and a knife in her chest. Her social security cheques had been rifled through. The next victim was 66 year-old June Roberts. Roberts knew Dana Sue Gray and was apparently helping her with alcohol addiction. Gray strangled Roberts with a telephone cord and stole two credit cards before going to a big shopping trip at the local mall. She treated the young son of her boyfriend to a meal, had a perm and manicure, then purchased some earrings, cowboy boots, a jacket, and some vodka. Gray even got some treats for her dog on the credit cards of the woman she had just murdered!

The last victim was 87 year-old Dora Beebe, who Gray attacked and killed in her usual fashion. Once again she went on a big spending spree with the credit cards she found in the victim's home. Unbelievably, Gray then tried to kill a woman named Dorinda Hawkins in an antiques store. Hawkins, who worked in the store, was helping Gray find some items when she suddenly felt some rope around her neck. Thankfully she managed to struggle and survive the attack. Dana Sue Gray was eventually arrested for the credit card theft and - of course - murder. She tried to pretend that she had merely stolen the credit cards and hadn't killed anyone but that was obviously a lie. Gray told the police that she was simply addicted to shopping and buying things. It was the only thing that made her happy. Shopping made her so happy that she was perfectly willing to murder people to get the money to fund her hobby. In 1998 she was sentenced to life in prison. Dana Sue Gray pleaded guilty to avoid the death penalty and was incarcerated in the California Women's Prison in

Chowchilla.

Felícitas Sánchez Aguillón was born in Cerro Azul, Veracruz, Mexico in 1890. Her terrible infamy lent her a number of titles - the most common of which are The Female Ripper of Colonia Roma and The Human Crusher of Little Angels. As a young woman she became a nurse although she was not the most maternal of people. She got married and had twin daughters but she was so indifferent to her children she arranged to have them adopted. Aguillón eventually moved to Mexico City where she began performing illegal abortions and got involved in the baby farming trade. Any babies that she couldn't get any money for she simply killed. She would drug or strangle the unwanted babies and then dump them in a river or sewer. The babies in her care were treated abominably. She made them sleep on the floor and fed them food that had gone off. They were given cold baths.

The awful crimes of Aguillón were uncovered in 1941 when the building in the Roma neighbourhood where she was based began to experience problems with its drains. Plumbers were sent to rectify the problem and they found things that were grisly and disturbing beyond words. In the pipe they found rotted meat and greased and bloodied rags. They also found a human skull that belonged to a baby. Aguillón is believed to have murdered between forty and fifty babies. She was able to keep her wicked scheme secret for as long as she did because one of her accomplices was a plumber. In the end though the drains simply became too clogged. Neighbours are said to have become suspicious of Aguillón because a thick pungent black smoke would sometimes come from her rooms. This was clearly a result of her burning the bodies of her victims. Aguillón would sometimes chop the babies up after she had killed them and hide them on garbage dumps.

When the police searched the rooms of Felícitas Sánchez Aguillón they found a number of religious artefacts and photographs of children. She had fled with a lover but thankfully was captured a day later. Felícitas Sánchez Aguillón was found to be a delusional woman who seemed to think she was on some sort of religious mission. She was clearly not the full shilling. Aguillón retreated into a childlike state in custody as the investigation developed. It was said that Aguillón had some baby adoption clients who were famous and involved in politics. The authorities were eager to get these names but Aguillón committed suicide by an overdose before the full details of her baby farming business were gathered. She was 50 years old. Aguillón had another daughter and husband by the time of her death. Her husband was convicted of being an accomplice and her daughter was placed in foster care. By any standards, Felícitas Sánchez Aguillón was one of the most heartless killers imaginable.

Benjamin Geen worked as a nurse at the Horton General Hospital in Banbury, Oxfordshire. During his time there, he was accused of administering lethal doses of medication to vulnerable patients in the acute care setting. Concern began when there was a notable cluster of unexplained deaths and medical emergencies on his shifts. The investigation into Geen's actions began after a series of suspicious incidents, including the sudden deterioration of several patients under his care. Eighteen patients suffered unexplained respiratory arrests while staff nurse Ben Geen was on duty. Medical staff became concerned about the patterns of these events, which seemed to coincide with Geen's presence on duty. Further inquiry revealed that Geen had been found to have unsupervised access to medications, which raised red flags. As the investigation unfolded, it became clear that he had a history of poor performance and had faced previous complaints regarding his conduct as a nurse. In 2007,

Benjamin Geen was arrested and charged with the murder of two patients — both elderly men — and the attempted murder of several others.

The trial commenced in 2008, where prosecutors argued that he had deliberately harmed patients achieving a level of control over the medical outcomes in which he was involved. In March 2008, Geen was convicted of the murders and attempted murder and sentenced to life in prison. The judge stressed the betrayal of trust and the gruesome nature of his actions, as he had taken advantage of his role in the healthcare system to perform these heinous acts. The thing which sealed Geen's doom was him turning up for work at the hospital and being arrested. They found he had a syringe in his coat with the dangerous muscle relaxant vecuronium. Vecuronium was found in one of the patients who had died. Geen's jacket also had residue of midazolam - a drug which had been illegally used on another victim. Geen claimed that he must have left the syringe in his coat by mistake after work but this rather weak excuse was not believed by the police nor a jury. Hospital syringes are used once but Geen's 'personal' syringe had been used more than once. Geen pointedly tried to hide the syringe and stop it being discovered.

Benjamin Geen was judged to have 'hero complex' by those who wrote reports on him. The term "hero complex" refers to a psychological condition in which a person feels an overwhelming need to be seen as a hero or saviour. Other staff at the hospital said Geen would get excited when a patient started crashing. Geen's barrister is none other than Mark McDonald. Mr McDonald is convinced that Geen is innocent and used (you guessed it) statistics in the (failed) appeal to argue that Geen's proximity to the emergency situations was not out of the ordinary and proved nothing. In this, Mark McDonald was backed by a number of statisticians

(Professor Jane Hutton, Professor Norman Fenton etc) now casting doubt on the Letby case. See what I mean about statisticians sometimes giving you the impression that they don't believe medical serial killers exist and no one is ever guilty? The Court of Appeal wasn't interested in the statistical evidence because they had solid evidence elsewhere - like the syringe. What about the syringe Mr McDonald? Mark McDonald said he used to work in a hospital and often unwittingly left with syringes in his pocket. What about the syringe having vecuronium Mr McDonald? Oh, it was probably an error or stitch up. The syringe was broken and empty. What about Ben Geen trying to hide the syringe Mr McDonald? Well, he knew he shouldn't be carrying it. But that doesn't make him guilty. Cos statistics and all that.

THE CASE FOR LUCY LETBY

Imagine for a moment this scenario. Lucy Letby is innocent. She never harmed any of those infants and this was all a miscarriage of justice. So you have this young woman, still in her early thirties, sitting in prison (with no prospect of ever being released) for crimes she didn't commit. Not only that but the crimes she was convicted for are the worst crimes you can imagine. What could possibly be more evil than baby killing? It is hard to think of a more nightmarish situation for someone to find themselves trapped in. Letby is, as far as the justice system is concerned, the modern day equivalent of monsters like Amelia Dyer and the Finchley Baby Farmers. Officially, Letby is one of the worst killers in recent history. A truly evil and heartless person who did things so awful we really can't comprehend them. Maybe this is part of the reason why not everyone thinks she is guilty. It just doesn't add up. How could this smiling dedicated nurse have done these terrible things?

Amelia Dyer became known as the Reading Baby Farmer and the Angel Maker for her crimes in Victorian England. Dyer worked as a 'baby farmer' - this involved looking after illegitimate babies in the hope that someone might adopt them one day. Dyer decided that she could keep all the money she was paid to do this for herself if she just murdered the babies and didn't have to incur any expenses looking after them. It is estimated that she killed 400 babies. Amelia Dyer is one of the most evil people that ever lived. On Wednesday the 10th of June 1896, she was hanged by James Billington at Newgate prison. The case of Amelia Dyer made Victorian England rethink the policy of 'baby farming' and introduce stricter laws when it came to foster care and adoption. Dyer's insanity was difficult to predict though because she was a trained nurse and someone who seemed (on the face of it) perfectly qualified to look after babies.

Amelia Sach (born 1873) and Annie Walters (born 1869) were two women who became known as The Finchley Baby Farmers. These two women conspired to murder babies in order to make money from the Victorian practice of baby farming. Amelia Sach started a business where babies who needed adoption could be left with her for a fee. Annie Walters would then poison the babies and dispose of them. Sach was married and a fairly respected woman (at least to the unsuspecting world at large) while much less is known about the background of Walters. Walters was deemed to be of very low intelligence and was the one who did the 'dirty work' in this evil scheme. Many of the babies that these two women dealt with were said to be the illegitimate children of servant girls and maids. There was a great stigma to having a child out of wedlock in the Victorian era and this created a need for women to look after unwanted infants until a home could be found for them.

This allowed evil women like Amelia Dyer and the Finchley Baby Farmers to take advantage. They would collect the fee for taking in a baby and then kill the baby so that they didn't incur any further expense looking after them. It should be noted though that the vast majority of baby farmers were kind and decent women who looked after the babies as if they were their own children. The likes of Sach and Walters and Dyer were tragic aberrations. What made it quite difficult to weed out murderous baby farmers was the fact that in this era a lot of infants and children died of disease or illness anyway. If an infant died, although tragic, it wasn't something that was especially uncommon. The hangman who executed Sach and Walters later wrote - 'These two women were baby farmers of the worst kind and were both repulsive in type. They had literally to be carried to the scaffold and protested to the end against their sentences.' The bodies of Amelia Sach and Annie Walters were buried in Holloway Prison after their execution. When the prison was rebuilt in 1971, the bodies had to be exhumed and moved elsewhere.

What if Lucy Letby is completely innocent and unwelcome comparisons to Dyer, Hindley, and all those awful monsters of the past are erroneous? As far as miscarriages of justice go this would be up there as one of the worst in recent criminal history. It would probably become the famous criminal miscarriage of all in Britain if Letby ever had her convictions quashed and was released. Everyone would always remember the terrible case of the innocent nurse who was wrongly convicted of murdering infants. This is one of but many factors in why there are a number of people who are still protesting against the convictions. If you believe that Letby is innocent then the thought of her sitting in prison for the rest of her life for crimes she didn't commit is horrible. Those who are doubtful about the verdict would say, given the stakes involved, why not put the evidence to the test again? In this chapter we will take a look at the evidence for why Letby could be innocent and seek to understand why a number of people seem to have serious doubts about her convictions. This chapter will therefore adopt a very staunch 'pro-Letby' stance and examine some of the possible reasons for doubt.

The place where many start in this regard is the Countess of Chester Hospital. In 2014, the Department of Health (DH) and NHS England gave the hospital a very bad rating in a report. 'Safety incidents include medical errors resulting in injury, suffering, disability or death in patients and failure to protect NHS whistle-blowers when they raise the alarm. Targets include potential underreporting of patient safety incidents, possible underreporting of incidents leading to death or severe harm and potential under-reporting of accidents which resulted in no harm.' The hospital where Letby worked was not exactly an NHS flagship. It was the medical equivalent of one of those rundown secondary schools which finishes in a mediocre position when it comes to GCSE results. It is certainly not outlandish to propose this hospital suffered from some serious care failings when Lucy Letby worked there. We have seen similar sorts of issues (a spike in deaths) at other hospitals but these hospitals didn't conclude that a serial killer was roaming the rooms murdering patients. Their focus was on the care issues in the hospital which led to this situation.

The hospital in Chester, in a desperate attempt to avoid calling the police and having to put up with media scrutiny, instigated some reports and investigations in the spike in deaths on the neonatal unit. These investigations were half-hearted, confused, and often truncated. They lacked forensic post-mortems and retesting. Dr Jane Hawden, a highly respected expert, was one of the people asked to do investigate but she did not come back and tell them they probably had a serial killer loose in the hospital. If it was so obvious to Dr Evans that this was a serial killer case why did so many other people fail to spot this? The instances of infant death at the hospital declined sharply when Letby was taken off duty. Supporters of Letby would point out though that the neonatal unit stopped accepting high risk babies after the rash of deaths and internal turmoil over Letby. There has been enough evidence by now to state with a reasonable degree of certainty that the Countess of Chester Hospital sometimes had trouble with staffing levels. The most salient aspect of this in relation to the case of Lucy Letby is that doctors were not always available to do rounds. This sometimes left more inexperienced doctors in charge and on call. This is not an ideal situation.

The case against Lucy Letby was circumstantial and no one actually saw her doing anything. The person who came closest to this was, as we talked about in earlier chapters, Dr Jayaram with the incident where he alleged he walked in on Letby just standing over a baby as it crashed and not doing anything to help. Supporters of Lucy Letby would point out that Dr Jayaram, despite later claiming that he had caught Letby in a very suspicious scenario, did not at the time report this incident to anyone at the hospital or mention it in his medical notes. He did not speak to Lucy Letby about the incident. If he had caught Lucy Letby 'in the act' why didn't he go to the police or immediately report this incident to his bosses? The reason why he didn't take immediate action is that he couldn't be certain of what he had seen and what was happening. This means he didn't catch Letby 'red-handed' as the prosecution claimed. Letby said she was giving the baby a moment to correct itself because this is what she had been taught to do as standard practice.

It is probably true to say that most of the nursing staff were bemused by the allegations against Letby and never saw her do anything which would constitute criminality or foul play in the neonatal unit. Letby has nurse friends who believe she is innocent but were not permitted to openly speak about the case out of fear it might damage their career. Lucy Letby's friends, ones she has known for years, also appear bemused by the convictions. Dawn, a woman who has known Letby since secondary school, told the Daily Mail that 'We know she couldn't have done anything that she's accused of, so without a doubt we stand by her. I grew up with Lucy and not a single thing that I've ever seen or witnessed of Lucy would let me for a moment believe she is capable of the thing's she's accused of. It is the most out of character accusation that you could ever put against Lucy. Think of your most kind gentle soft friend and think that they're being accused of harming babies.' Dawn believes that the criminal case against Letby was designed to fit a theory and did not consider all possibilities.

Some nurses have said that they don't set much store in the fact that Letby was found to have medical handover sheets from the hospital at her home. One nurse told the media that taking home handover sheets by accident is something that all nurses have done. The post-it-notes in which Letby seemed to be offering a rambling form of confession were apparently written on the advice of a counsellor and yet this was not mentioned at the original trial. The criminologist David Wilson has said that he thinks the post-it-notes are irrelevant to the case and no indication or anything - let alone guilt. It should be mentioned too that in one of her private notes, which were treated as confessions in the media, Letby wrote 'there is obviously no evidence' on one of them. If she was a serial killer, Letby having all those handover sheets (only a small minority were related to the infants in the convictions) and Facebook searches on the families does seem odd in respect of the fact that Letby is plainly intelligent and yet left herself in a situation where she had all these apparent links to the case. If she was really a calculating serial killer wouldn't she have made sure there was no evidence like this at her home or on her computer?

If she was really a serial killer, why did Letby make such a fuss when they began the process of removing her from the unit? Wasn't this simply drawing attention to herself? Perhaps she made such a fuss because she was innocent and angered by her treatment. The suspicion around Lucy Letby in the hospital arose as a result of the fact that she always seemed to be on duty when one of these emergencies occurred. Supporters of Letby have pointed out there were deaths in the unit during this time which were not publicised or attributed to Letby at the trial. This would render the 'bad things only happened when Lucy was there' theory questionable. The media and even Dr Evans suggested after the trial that Letby was probably responsible for many more deaths beyond her original convictions. If this is the case why have there been no charges for these other murders and attacks? Where are they? Those who don't believe Letby is guilty could point to the fact that the post-mortems did not have any coroners rushing to announce there was a medical serial killer in Chester. A coroner ascribed natural causes (insufficient blood flow in the womb) in the case of Child C but Letby was later charged with this infant's murder after Dr Evans decided it had been deliberately harmed. Why did the coroner fail to spot evidence of deliberate harm if this was so obvious to Dr Evans?

The police examined the computers and devices of Lucy Letby after her arrest to scrutinise details of her online and messaging activity. It was through this process that evidence of her searching the families of infants on Facebook was found. However, what was not found by the police was any evidence that Letby had done any online research on air embolisms or insulin poisoning or any medical method of murder at all. There were no medical serial killer searches either. Lucy Letby, as a person, is something of an anomaly when it comes to serial killers because she didn't tick any of the boxes usually cited as common in such killers. She had a good upbringing, friends and a social life, no criminal record, no issues with drugs or alcohol, no relationship troubles. To believe she is guilty we must believe that she did all this work to become a nurse merely to have the chance to murder babies. Either that or she woke up one day and suddenly decided to become a serial killer. To do what Letby was convicted of doing you'd have to be highly disturbed and yet there is zero evidence from her life that Letby was unhinged or disturbed or had any dark secrets in her closet.

The Journal of Investigative Psychology and Offender Profiling, in a study, found that medical serial killers frequently switch hospitals and work in different places - presumably to decrease their chances of drawing attention to themselves and being detected. This though did not apply to Lucy Letby. Letby was dogged in her determination to stay at Chester - even when the allegations against her began to bubble. If she was a serial killer why was she stupid enough to stay at the same hospital and attract suspicion? The study found that medical serial killers tend to have a lot of disciplinary problems but this was not the case with Letby. If anything she was seen as a model nurse in that she was dedicated and happy to do extra shifts. The study also found that the vast majority of medical serial killers had a history of mental instability and depression. This is yet another thing which didn't really apply to Lucy Letby. Her friends all described her as a normal and fun loving person. Medical serial killers will typically stick to one specific method of murder - the method they judge is least likely to be detected. Lucy Letby on the other hand was accused of injecting air, insulin poisoning, dislodging breathing tubes, and over-feeding. Why would she be stupid enough to do all these different things and increase her chances of detection?

The former neonatologist Dr Hall (who we have previously mentioned in this book) doesn't believe Lucy Letby had a fair trial because there were no medical witnesses called by the defence to offer an alternative viewpoint to the air embolism theories of Dr Evans and others. The jury in the trial only heard one side of the story when it came to the medical details in this case. Ben Myers KC doggedly questioned the medical evidence in court and offered alternative explanations but Myers is a barrister with no medical background or qualifications. To hear these alternative viewpoints coming not from a barrister but a respected medical professional like Dr Hall would have added another dimension of complexity to the trial and given the jury much more to think about. It would have made the trial more balanced and Letby's defence stronger.

The fact that no medical witnesses were called by the defence at Lucy Letby's trial, presumably due to tactical reasons, has also led many others argue that the trial wasn't fair. Though the court system states that witnesses are bound to the court rather than one side or the other and must be impartial we know this isn't quite the case. The prosecution is not going to put someone in the witness box who might potentially disagree with all their prosecution evidence. The same goes for the defence. So if experts had testified for the defence at the trial then at least there would have been a counter to the prevailing tide coming from the other direction. So we ended up with Ben Myers KC having to question doctors on medical matters and try to trip them up. Though well briefed for sure,

Ben Myers is a barrister not a doctor. If the defence had put Dr Michael Hall in the witness box he would, under questioning by Ben Myers, been able to dispute some of the salient theories being used by the prosecution to convict Lucy Letby.

There is no guarantee this would have altered the verdict and the defence would not have relished Dr Hall being cross-examined by the prosecution but at the very least it would have given the jury something to think about if there was a respected doctor offering some plausible alternative theories to the prosecution. "What you have, when you don't have defence experts," Letby's new barrister Mark McDonald told Channel 5, "is prosecution experts going pretty much unchallenged. So you're left there with this expert's evidence hanging, with no other experts saying: "Actually, that can't be right". It leads, almost certainly, to the inevitable consequence that that someone's going to be convicted. I know, having been involved in numerous child abuse cases, how difficult it is to get an expert in this country to help you. They won't." A nurse who worked with Lucy Letby has since said she wanted to be a character witness for Letby at the trial but the NHS and police blocked her from doing this.

Since the Letby trial some doctors have pointed out that it is very difficult sometimes to pinpoint why a baby has died and it is not unusual for an infant death to be officially unexplained when it comes to precise medical causes. In the case of the Countess of Chester Hospital, a spike in unexplained infant deaths was eventually judged to be foul play by a combination of methods - primarily air embolism. Since the trial a number of doctors and experts have disputed this theory and told the media that they certainly wouldn't have come up with these conclusions had they been in the shoes of Dr Evans (the chief prosecution witness and the man who basically built the whole criminal case against Letby). The biggest bone of contention for medical critics is the air embolism theory which Dr Evans cited as the cause in a number of cases when he was asked to review the Countess of Chester neonatal unit death/emergency spike by Cheshire Police. The field of air embolism study is somewhat vague in that there are few people who are recognised as experts. Dr Dewi Evans certainly wasn't an expert himself when it came to this area of medicine.

In simple terms, a number of medical professionals have stated that, in their view, the air embolism theory of Dr Evans in relation to the Letby case is baffling and misguided. Dr Svilena Dimitrova, a consultant neonatologist who has been openly critical of the Letby trial, told the media that if a baby had been injected with lots of air (which in and of itself is, say Letby supporters, a difficult and time consuming thing to do - which makes some believe it isn't realistic as a method of murder) a competent team of doctors would have immediately diagnosed this and simply aspirated the air out. Dr Dimitrova would therefore, and she is not alone in this, find it implausible to think that Dr Dewi Evans, who has been retired since 2009, would be able to immediately diagnose something second hand which all the doctors and consultants in the hospital missed at the time. Other medical professionals have pointed out too that air in an infant is sometimes a natural consequence of ventilation and resuscitation and it is a tremendous leap of logic to attribute this fact to foul play.

Critics of Dr Evans have complained about his comments that in the absence of any other explanation he concluded it could only be air embolisms. This process of elimination is illogical because if you rule out other things it doesn't automatically follow that one specific thing you haven't got around to yet is to blame. One of the conclusions of Dr Evans was that in some cases Lucy Letby had injected air via nasogastric tubes as a method of murder. Some medical professionals have disputed this conclusion and pointed out that nasogastric tubes are so minuscule that it would take several refills to do this. Even if a killer somehow found all the time to secretly do this in a busy hospital the air could then be negated by the baby breaking wind or burping. A number of medical experts therefore simply don't buy the central theory which was used as the central plank in the prosecution and conviction of Lucy Letby. If, as some believe, the air embolism theory is mistaken, then this basically torpedoes most of the case against Letby and leaves what remains highly questionable too. If the air embolism theory is wrong then this removes most of the murders or attacks attributed to Letby and almost certainly means she wasn't a killer and a big mistake has been made.

Those who are dubious about the convictions might also argue that the Countess of Chester Hospital was very busy when Letby worked there and had more infants than usual to look after. Given the problems the hospital had when it came to maintaining a high standard of care we can see how a theory might be proposed where the neonatal unit found itself in a situation where it was in over its head looking after a number of premature babies who required very acute care. In this scenario the spike in deaths can be logically explained and Lucy Letby was wrongly singled out as the problem simply because she worked a lot of extra shifts on account of needing the money because she had purchased a house. Some statisticians might say that Lucy Letby was therefore doomed simply by going to work a lot. If she hadn't purchased a house and didn't do all those extra shifts there probably would have been no suspicion at all because Letby wouldn't have been there half the time. There was an incident at the Countess of Chester hospital not long before Letby worked there where an infant died because a nasogastric tube was applied incorrectly. This was far from the only incident where the hospital had trouble with tubes when it came to babies. The general theory is that inexperienced staff were to blame.

With this in mind, one could imagine a scenario where dislodged or incorrectly applied tubes were mistakes rather than deliberate - including those attributed to Lucy Letby. One of the parents from the Letby case said he saw one of the doctors in the Chester hospital "... look up how to perform the chest drain and where the incisions and tubes should go. It looked as though they were following a tutorial and not as if they really knew what they were doing." That's not going to inspire much confidence is it? Doctors googling medical procedures as they perform them. They are supposed to know this stuff. A doctor who is a bit foggy on how to do a chest drain shouldn't really be doing one in the first place. A number of medical studies have indicated that a surprisingly high number of infant deaths are unexplained. With this in mind, it is a leap to attribute a number of unexplained infant deaths to one person. Critics of Letby's convictions have also argued that the babies were not nearly as stable as Dr Evans claimed they were at the trial. "It's my opinion," said Dr Hall, "the prosecution medical expert witnesses exaggerated the degree of wellness of those babies to a significant extent. I would have thought it would have had a significant influence on the jury. One example of this is Baby A. His vital signs were displayed to the court on several occasions and it was clear that he was receiving respiratory support. But his breathing rate was clearly abnormal for almost 24 hours, or at least intermittently, certainly for the last 12 hours before he collapsed."

Which brings us back to the crux of the whole debate - the stability of the infants. Some believe that the babies were not as stable as the prosecution argued and when you factor in possible sub-optimal care then you have an explanation which is more plausible than the theory that a serial killer nurse was at large in the unit. Letby's proximity to the deaths of emergencies is disputed by some in that the wider statistical picture is uncertain (or, some might argue, ignored) but there is also the fact that Letby was more qualified than some other nurses and worked extra shifts. With this mind it is not so strange she usually seemed to be on duty when something happened. Some statisticians have argued that one could construct a mathematical model in which every nurse in the Chester neonatal unit could be made to look suspicious in relation to the duty rota. The statistician Professor Jane Hutton of Warwick University, who was one of the 24 'experts' who wanted the Thirwall Inquiry postponed, was actually going to help the police in the Letby investigation but then had her services dispensed with. Why? Is it because she didn't agree with their conclusions? Of the police, Hutton said, "The work was done with Lucy Letby in mind, which is completely inappropriate. In a highly complex case like this, there are very high standards and it's not clear whether they've been followed."

At the original trial of Lucy Letby, Dr Dewi Evans (the chief prosecution witness) said in his evidence that Child C died by injection of air. His theory was that a bubble of air had made it impossible for the infant to breathe. Dr Evans based this on an X-ray he had seen. However, in 2024, Dr Evans said he had changed his mind about Child C and the bubble of air didn't kill the infant. He now declared that the infant was killed by air in the stomach in a fresh attack the next day. Some have pointed out that that Letby wasn't on duty in the timeline of the original diagnosis of the air bubble by Dr Evans. In other words, Letby had no contact with the baby when the X-ray (which Dr Evans based his original theory upon) was taken. Critics of Dr Evans and the convictions would want to know why he was allowed to change some of his evidence a year after the trial with no repercussions and perhaps question too whether he was adjusting his theories to line Letby up more squarely in the timeline.

Proffessor Colin Morely, a retired professor of neonatology from the University of Cambridge, told BBC radio that he believes Child C died of natural causes - most likely a bowel obstruction. Morely was critical of the 'very strange' theories of Dr Evans. Dr Michael Hall, who was frustrated not to be called by the defence to give evidence at the Letby trial, told the BBC that in his view the X-ray of Child C did not show any evidence of deliberate harm and the excess gas in the infant has a number of natural explanations considerably more plausible than the serial killer nurse theory of the prosecution. In the trial of Letby, Child O was judged to have suffered a blunt trauma to the liver likened to a car crash. A pathologist, who did wish to be named, told the BBC this was a ridiculous assertion. The pathologist said the tests on Child O displayed natural symptoms she had seen herself at least three times. It was these medical counter views which were missing from the trial. Letby's defence would clearly have been enhanced by other medical experts casting doubt on the conclusions drawn by the prosecution from the medical evidence in the case.

The two cases of insulin poisoning that Letby was convicted of were the most difficult when it came to her defence. The jury found it much easier to reach a verdict on these specific convictions than others. Letby agreed with Nick Johnson QC in court that insulin poisoning had happened but said it wasn't her. This was one of the worst moments of the trial for the defence. Critics of the Letby conviction, when it comes to insulin, will sometimes reference Professor Alan Wayne Jones - a retired forensic toxicologist. Jones is critical of the immunoassay method which was used in the cases of Letby and Colin Norris. Immunoassays are biochemical tests which use the specificity of antibodies to detect and quantify substances (like insulin) in a sample. Prof Alan Wayne Jones, and others, have argued that a higher clinical standard of testing should be required in criminal cases. Dr Adel Ismail was also critical of the insulin testing method used in the Letby case. "Of all the technologies we use in the lab for measurements, the one with the highest error rate is the immunoassay and this is usually due to interference in an individual sample," said Dr Ismail. "A patient's blood can contain antibodies with 10 billion different permutations that by sheer chance can interact with the test, causing falsely high or falsely low results and these results can be extreme."

Professor Geoff Chase, from the University of Canterbury in New Zealand, told the BBC that a much higher dose of insulin would be required to cause harm than the test results of the babies Letby was convicted of poisoning indicated. Professor Chase, who has studied how insulin works in babies for many years, therefore argues that the convictions in the cases of Child F and Child L would need to be supported by evidence that a very large amount of insulin went missing in the hospital when Letby worked there. There is no reported evidence though that a very large amount of insulin did go missing. Dr Charline Bottinelli, an insulin expert from the Laboratoire LAT Lumtox, has said that the insulin incidents in the Letby case could be explained by insulinoma or hypoglycaemia. Some believe it was unfair that Letby was cross-examined about the insulin cases at the trial because it was impossible for her to answer these complex questions. All she could do was listen to Nick Johnson say that insulin poisoning had taken place and then insist that (if this was the case) it wasn't her. This made it look like Letby was admitting insulin poisoning had taken place but was blaming someone else. If she was innocent though Letby would be clueless about the alleged insulin poisoning and what happened in relation to this so her confusion - taken for guilt - would be genuine.

Critics of the convictions might ask how Letby tampered with nutrient bags without anyone noticing. What happened to the nutrient bags? Where was the evidence? If she is a killer, why did she switch to a different murder method and one which had more chance of being detected? In the second insulin case in the prosecution case against Letby, far less insulin was used than in the first. Why? If she was a medical serial killer and poisoner why would Letby use less insulin the second time? There was a third possible insulin poisoning in the Countess of Chester Hospital in November 2015. The infant in question (happily) survived and recovered. Alder Hey Hospital diagnosed hyperinsulinism - an excessive secretion of insulin from the pancreas which can lead to low blood sugar (hypoglycemia). Dr Dewi Evans did not agree with this diagnosis. Nonetheless, this case did not feature in the trial and Lucy Letby was not blamed - despite its similarities to the two other insulin cases in her trial. Was this case dropped because Alder Hey had provided an alternative (alternative to murder that is) explanation which would have weakened the prosecution case on the two insulin incidents Letby was convicted of?

Critics of the Letby conviction might point out the Texas sharpshooter fallacy and accuse Dr Evans of something similar. The Texas sharpshooter fallacy is a logical fallacy that occurs when an individual or group disregards random data and instead identifies patterns or connections that conform to their desired conclusion while ignoring data that contradicts it. The name is derived from a hypothetical scenario in which a sharpshooter fires at a barn, and then paints a target around the bullet holes to make it look like they are accurate shots. In essence, this fallacy highlights a flawed reasoning process in which one cherry-picks data points that support a specific argument while neglecting other relevant information that might provide a different picture. It is often seen in the context of pseudoscience, statistics, and argumentation, where selective data usage can lead to misleading conclusions.

We could ask ourselves this in closing - what would have happened if Cheshire Police had hired Dr Michael Hall to review the cases for the investigation rather than Dr Evans? Would there even have been a trial? The simple fact is that babies, tragically, can die unexpectedly. Emergencies and collapses in a baby unit are far from unheard of or uncommon. Could it be that this natural fact combined with a less than stellar hospital resulted in an unlucky streak which found an innocent nurse wrongly implicated in foul play? Former staff at the hospital have spoken about infections, poor conditions, broken equipment, and low staff morale. Is it not more plausible to think that all of these things and more were responsible for spike in deaths and emergencies at the neonatal unit? The alternative is that a nurse suddenly went beserk and turned into a serial killer. Which of those two theories sounds more realistic? As you can see, it isn't difficult to paint a narrative and come up with any number of reasons for why the convictions of Lucy Letby are questionable to some observers. In the next chapter we will become the prosecution rather than the defence and examine the case for Letby being guilty.

THE CASE AGAINST LUCY LETBY

So now comes prosecution rebuttal to the reasons why Letby might be innocent. In this chapter, as a contrary exercise to the last chapter, we shall be pro-conviction and attempt to build a case for why she is guilty. Let us begin with the main themes of the Letby is Innocent collective. The two recurring themes are that (1) Letby was made a scapegoat for NHS failings and (2) there is no evidence to prove she is guilty. Straight away we have a very obvious problem. If there is no evidence how can Lucy Letby be a scapegoat? Surely, if one were to pin this all on a scapegoat you'd want evidence wouldn't you? These things can't both be true. Secondly, if Lucy Letby was an innocent victim of hospital failings and doctors and the hospital trying to protect its reputation this makes the consultants and prosecution witnesses both insane and evil. The conspiracy angle just doesn't add up. The more plausible theory is that these consultants genuinely think Letby is guilty and acted upon that and gave evidence accordingly.

And these consultants, whatever you might have read in the New Yorker and Science on Trial (rest in peace), are not bungling idiots who routinely accuse nurses of being serial killers. They are actually real doctors and real medical professionals. The credentials of those who were involved in investigating Letby are no less valid than those now debating the convictions. In most cases they are more valid. Another problem with the Letby as patsy/scapegoat theory is that the hospital went to extreme lengths to give Letby the benefit of the doubt and avoid taking any action. The police were only called in when the suspicions concerning Letby became too nagging and persistent to ignore. Another thing which doesn't make any sense is that if this was all a big conspiracy for the benefit of the hospital's reputation how is not noticing there was a serial killer working in the neonatal unit preferable to admitting a few care failings?

It is quite frequently mentioned that the hospital in Chester had trouble with pseudomonas when Letby worked there. This is often cited as a potential explanation for the tragic spike in baby deaths. David Davies and John Sweeney have both mentioned this in their respective comments on why they think Letby might innocent. Pseudomonas aeruginosa is a gram-negative bacterium that is commonly found in various environments, including soil, water, and as part of the normal flora of humans. It is an opportunistic pathogen known for its versatility and resistance to many antibiotics, making it a significant cause of infections, particularly in hospital settings. The problem with the infection theory is that special safety filters were put on the taps in the baby unit two months before Letby's 'killing spree' began. The other problem with the infection theory is that more than one consultant has testified that they considered this theory for themselves but upon investigation found no medical evidence that any of the infants showed symptoms of an infection of this type.

Contrary to what you might have read online, the consultants and doctors in the Countess of Chester Hospital were not imbeciles. They were well aware that infections can occur in hospitals and so tested this theory for themselves. If they'd found evidence of an infection problem they would have said so. It would now be a matter of public record rather than an online conspiracy theory. Are we to believe they pretended there was a serial killer to avoid admitting an infection problem? Seriously? The only witness called at the trial was a plumber named Lorenzo Mansutti, who worked at the hospital. At some point in the trial, Letby suddenly began talking about plumbing and sewage and dubiously suggested this was a factor in the infant emergencies. However, Nick Johnson KC established that Letby never mentioned plumbing once in her police interviews and never filled in a single Datix form complaining about plumbing and sewage when she worked as a nurse. If this sewage and plumbing problem was of such legendary proportions according to some of Letby's supporters why did Letby herself never complain about it when she actually worked in the hospital?

Under cross-examination, the plumber Mr Mansutti agreed that most of the sewage incidents didn't affect the neonatal unit and there was never an occasion when fresh safe water wasn't available. If this hospital, as some Letby supporters allege, had a medieval style sewage problem why did it only affect the neonatal unit? Why weren't other patients in the hospital suddenly falling ill or showing signs of infection? "As far as the sewage problem is concerned," Dr Evans told the John Sweeney podcast, "I don't know when this occurred. If there was a sewage problem, it would not explain what caused the death of these babies. If any of the babies had acquired pseudomonas [bacteria] septicemia, you would expect them to deteriorate over a period of time as the pseudomonas got hold, and that would lead to significant changes in their clinical status – the need for more oxygen, irregular breathing habits, deterioration in oxygen saturation, blood tests becoming abnormal, changes in skin colour. Several of these babies were resuscitated successfully. What has the sewage problem got to do with the fact that seven babies were murdered and seven babies were the victims of attempted murder over a period of 13 months, where there was no evidence of pseudomonas infection or of a serious pathogenic infection in most of them?"

The biggest problem for Letby's defence and the closest thing in the case to a smoking gun concerns the two cases of insulin poisoning. Neither her barrister Ben Myers KC nor Letby disputed the poisoning. They simply said if poisoning happened it wasn't Letby. Since the trial, we've seen Letby supporters and some medical experts dispute the insulin cases mainly by criticising the immunoassay method used. The problem is that none of these critics had access to all the files, tests, and medical notes that those involved in the tests and trial did. And it isn't as if the immunoassay method is useless. It is rare for this method to be false. Keith Frayn, an emeritus professor of human metabolism at the University of Oxford, disputed the claims that the immunoassay insulin tests in the Letby case were unreliable. "I don't think many people who know about insulin assays would say you can disregard those tests," he said. "They are very clear." Professor Frayn believes the tests were outside the margin of error.

Dr Anna Milan is a biochemist who was at the Royal Liverpool Hospital where the insulin tests were carried out. She testified that the insulin was not natural and had been administered. Dr Gwen Wark, director of the RSCH Peptide Hormone Laboratory in Guildford (a prestigious institution), confirmed the accuracy of these tests in evidence. This was all then essentially peer reviewed by Professor Peter Hindmarsh, a paediatric endocrinologist who gave evidence at Letby's trial. If you think the insulin aspect to the Letby case was faulty or wrong or dodgy you are basically saying that Dr Anna Milan, the RSCH Peptide Hormone Laboratory, the emeritus professor of human metabolism at the University of Oxford, and Professor Peter Hindmarsh don't know what they are talking about and are all stupid. Either that or they were all part of the great conspiracy to scapegoat Letby.

The famous article in the New Yorker made great play of the Royal Liverpool Hospital not being sufficient (in criminal cases) for testing on whether synthetic insulin has been administered. That is true but the test WAS confirmed by Dr Gwen Wark, director of the RSCH Peptide Hormone Laboratory in Guildford - rendering the New Yorker complaint null and void. Further test were not carried out because the patients recovered. This is standard practice and not something sinister or suspicious. Dr Wolfsdorf, a professor at Harvard Medical School, was quoted in the Moritz/Coffey book about Lucy Letby that the insulin results in the Letby case were not faulty (as implied by him in the New Yorker article) but symptomatic of factitious hypoglycemia. Factitious hypoglycemia results from the surreptitious or accidental use of insulin or oral insulin secretagogues. The term factitious (or factitial) hypoglycemia is often used to indicate human activity - whether accidental or deliberate foul play. Dr Wolfsdorf had changed his mind after having access to more evidence. Those who prosecuted Letby would argue that if everyone had access to all the clinical records they would realise that Letby is guilty.

At the Thirwall Inquiry, Dr Anna Milan was easily able to debunk the online conspiracy theories which occasionally run rampant in relation to the insulin area of this case. The hospital in Chester went through six vials of insulin in 2015 - double the usual annual amount. Coincidence? There seem to be an awful lot of coincidences when it comes to Lucy Letby. Supporters of Letby often say that how could Letby know which infant would be dosed if she spiked a nutrient bag? This is simple. You select the bags according to the order they are arranged. So it wouldn't take a criminal genius to do this. At the trial, Lucy Letby said had no memory Child F's blood sugar level. She said she was unaware of this situation. But the police had evidence of texts in which Letby discussed the blood sugar level of the infant with a colleague and suggested an endocrine problem. We saw this pattern more than once. Letby suggesting an alternative medical problem for an infant. Why did she do this? The obvious answer is misdirection.

At her police interview, Letby asked if they had tested the

nutrient bags. She knew full well that the nutrient bags were discarded. Letby was essentially, in a tactical move, requesting evidence that she knew didn't exist in order to paint herself in a more open and innocent light. The case against Letby was largely circumstantial but then most cases are. That's how you build a prosecution case. You build up a big picture of suspicious events which seem implausible as mere blanket coincidence. You have to tally up the circumstantial evidence and ascertain in which direction it is pointing. In this case it was all pointing at Lucy Letby. Let us now run through some of the little details which formed the building blocks of the case against Letby. There was the fact that the emergencies happened on the day shift when Letby worked days and then moved to the night shift when Letby worked nights. The deaths briefly stopped when Letby was on holiday in Ibiza. A member of staff told the Thirwall Inquiry that she noticed how a particular infant always seemed fine when Letby was not there and then suddenly ill when Letby was on shift. The emergencies flattened out when Letby was moved to a clerical job.

Lucy Letby's trial evidence was frequently at odds with the evidence she gave in her police interviews. She also disputed the evidence of Dr Jayaram, another nurse, and even the mother of one of the infants. Are we to believe that all these people are all liars and only Lucy Letby tells the truth? Why would the mother of one of the infants lie? Surely this mother's memory when it comes to her child is going to be better than that of Lucy Letby - who had other infants to look after at the time. And then there were the accounts of Letby seeming animated and excited when an infant died. And the nurse who said Letby said a baby looked pale when the lights were not even on and you couldn't see anything. This baby died the next day - at the hands of Letby according to the jury. Letby was also proven to have falsified some of her medical notes (example - Letby wrote that Child O had breathing support when this wasn't the case). She did numerous Facebook searches on the families of infants who had died. These included occasions when she looked at the Facebook of grieving families on Christmas Day and the anniversaries of their baby's deaths. Why would you do this?

Letby's post-it-notes might have been written on the suggestion of a GP or counsellor but they were still deeply odd and sinister with lines like "I am evil I did this." If I was ordered to write post-it-notes as therapy I certainly wouldn't be writing things like "I am a horrible evil person" or "I killed them on purpose" as Letby did. Lucy Letby also wrote a weird past tense note in relation to the triplets in which she acted as if they were all dead - despite one of them being alive. Letby had over 250 medical handover notes in her house. This included resuscitation data for one infant which had been scribbled on a paper towel. Letby had retrieved this piece of paper from a waste paper bin and taken it home. Why? It is often said that Letby, alarmingly normal, dorky even, ticks no standard serial killer boxes. Details of her conduct when she came under suspicion did though reveal more than a hint of narcissistic personality disorder. A personality disorder characterised by a life-long pattern of exaggerated feelings of self-importance, an excessive need for admiration, and a lack of empathy. We saw in Letby's emails to staff during her grievance procedure that she would instruct them on how they were supposed to treat her when she came back. Her behaviour when infants died was also odd at times. Don't take my word for it. This is what what some of the parents involved in the case said.

The main focus of Letby supporters seems to be Dr Dewi Evans - the chief prosecution witness. There have been a multitude of brickbats thrown in his direction since the trial. The general tone of the complaints are that Dr Evans is retired, out of touch, knows nothing about air embolisms, incompetent, and touted himself for the Letby investigation because he knew he'd get paid very well for his services. Ben Myers tried to get the evidence of Dr Evans thrown out half-way through the trial on the grounds that Evans was impartial and had no evidence for his theories. At worst the accusation against Dr Evans is that he embellished the possibility of foul play in Chester purely for financial gain - which is an outrageous suggestion. At best, the accusations against Dr Evans from Letby supporters are that he's an incompetent old fool who doesn't have the faintest idea what he is talking about when it comes to medicine. Here is the problem with all of this. Dr Evans designed a neonatal unit from scratch in the 1980s. This is his specialist area. He has looked after more babies than you've had hot dinners. Dr Evans spent forty odd years of his life working in infant care. He has forgotten more about neonatal care than most people will ever know.

Evans has also been a witness for the defence many times in criminal cases and once got a case thrown out because he didn't think there was any evidence. It isn't as if he trawls around the country looking for nurses to accuse of being serial killers. As for Dr Evans being retired from clinical practice, well, Dr Michael Hall, who is perhaps the most famous of the professionals who question the convictions, is also retired. So what? It isn't as if you instantly forget everything you ever learned once you retire. Much is made of Dr Evans not having much experience (Evans said there was a solitary case once in a hospital he worked at) of air embolisms. However, Dr Shoo Lee, who was put up as the great expert in this field at the appeal and by Letby supporters, doesn't have much experience of air embolisms either. He merely wrote a paper on the subject. Dr Lee's evidence was tossed out at the appeal because he was clueless about the fine details of the original trial and the medical records of the infants. The work of Dr Evans was also peer reviewed by other experts before the trial. It isn't as if he was the only person who the police consulted. Dr Bohin reviewed the cases independent of Dr Evans. She had access to imaging and clinical notes and reached similar conclusions.

Air embolisms are not, contrary to what some supporters of Letby have claimed, impossible to diagnose. It has also since come to light that Letby's defence had access to a radiologist, insulin expert, and coroner but all of these experts, once they had reviewed the evidence, decided that Letby was guilty and the prosecution was sound. Much is made by Letby supporters of Dr Michael Hall disputing the theories of Dr Evans. The thing is though that Dr Hall has admitted that he doesn't know if Letby is innocent. He has also admitted that he doesn't have all the answers and concedes that some parts of the Letby case are not easy to explain. He filed reports on all the cases in the Letby trial and did not declare that all of the deaths and collapses could be explained. In his reports he even said that air embolism could not be ruled out in some instances. As an expert to the defence (though not called to speak at the trial), Dr Hall sat in on meetings with the prosecution experts before the trial to find areas of this agreement. This might be why he wasn't called to give evidence. Nick Johnson KC could have simply asked Dr Hall in court about all the things he agreed on with the prosecution witnesses. After this, Johnson could have said 'no further questions' and sat down.

Some experts contend that it isn't that difficult at all to inject air into a nasogastric tube. The air embolism theory was generally agreed on at the trial by Professor Owen Arthurs, the radiologist at Great Ormond Street Hospital. Professor Arthurs testified that X-rays showed unusual columns of air in some of the infants. This was then agreed on by Dr Andreas Marnerides, an expert in neonatal pathology. Dr Marnerides testified that unexplained bubbles of air were present in the cases of Child A and Child D. Those who ridicule the air embolism theory tend to focus on Dr Evans. However, by doing this they are also essentially saying that Professor Owen Arthurs and Dr Andreas Marnerides are both clueless. So, are we seriously saying that all these people online ridiculing the air embolism theory know more about this subject than the highly respected radiologist at Great Ormond Street Hospital? I would contend that this is not a serious proposition. Critics of Dr Evans and the air embolism theory tend to focus on skin discolouration being weak and disputable as a diagnosis. But this was merely a small component of the prosecution case. Dr Andreas Marnerides also testified that he found air around the tip of one of the infant UVC catheters. And why has the hospital not experienced any of the strange skin mottling symptoms since Letby left?

There were 22 cases reviewed by the police for the criminal investigation. No other nurse was there for more than seven of these incidents. Letby on the other seemed to be there all the time for everything. Letby supporters of a statistical bent have said that the evidence is unfair because deaths or emergencies where Letby was not at the hospital were not included on the duty chart. This misses the point. Dr Evans had never heard of Lucy Letby when he investigated the hospital. He simply gave the police a list of deaths and collapses he judged to be suspicious or unexplained. The police compared this list to the duty rota and found that Lucy Letby was the biggest red flag because she always seemed to be there when something happened. If one believes in foul play (and not everyone does) then the prime suspect can only be Lucy Letby. To say that things sometimes happened when she wasn't there as if this was conviction shattering proof of innocence would be like saying there was an unsolved death in Bradford in 1980 so this must mean that Peter Sutcliffe wasn't the Yorkshire Ripper. If you go down the foul play road, as the authorities did, Lucy Letby was the only person who had the opportunity to commit these acts.

The rapid rate of collapse, recovery, and collapse (again) of the babies in the neonatal unit was not natural or normal. It baffled the doctors. While it is true that babies are fragile and vulnerable and unexplained deaths can occur this is not 1876. Modern neonatal units do not commonly lose patients by the half dozen in a matter of days and weeks. The spike in deaths was unusual and not something the doctors there considered normal. There were only two or three deaths a year before Letby and these were explained. At the trial of Lucy Letby, more than one doctor testified how baffled they were by apparently stable babies suddenly collapsing or worse. Aside from air embolisms and insulin, there was also evidence of over-feeding. So you've got all these different suspicious incidents where babies either collapsed unexpectedly or displayed evidence of foul play. This was all backed up by respected experts way beyond Dr Evans. You've got consultants in the hospital saying they were baffled by what was happening. You've got a nurse who was there a lot more than other nurses. You've got evidence of synthetic insulin being administered.

You've got the emergencies dovetailing with Letby's shift pattern. You've got a doctor, nurse, and mother all saying they saw Letby acting suspiciously. What is the alternative to Lucy Letby's guilt? Bad plumbing? A blocked sink? Unlucky coincidence? A lack of staff? A gigantic conspiracy involving the hospital and NHS? If you believe that Letby is innocent then that means that all the details we've mentioned connecting her to the case are pure coincidence and totally irrelevant. It also means that the doctors at the hospital and the medical professionals who gave evidence at the trial all got it completely wrong. All of them. None of this is impossible but it does seem rather unlikely. "Medical or scientific evidence in a case should never be compartmentalised or examined in isolation from the wider canvas," said Rachel Langdale KC at the Thirwall Inquiry. "Those who do this will be less likely to see the picture as a whole and in failing to see the picture as a whole, they may reach conclusions that are not only wrong but are speculative and damaging."

Child O and Child P were two of the triplet siblings born at 33 weeks gestation. This gave them a 99% chance of survival. And yet they mysteriously died. Dr David Harkness told the trial that Child A was completely stable until a sudden collapse. There was 38 other nurses working in the neonatal unit with Lucy Letby but none of them could be linked (in terms of their shifts) to the deaths and emergencies on anything approaching the frequency of Letby. Dr Andreas Marnerides testified that Child O's death was a result of an "inflicted traumatic injury to the liver". The general counter to this by Letby supporters that it was caused by vigorous CPR. Dr Marnerides was adamant this wasn't the case. "I have never seen this type of injury in the context of CPR," he said. Child E was the baby that the mother testified hearing screaming and upon investigating found Letby with the infant and blood around its mouth. Letby told the mother not to worry and to wait outside. The baby died the next day. In her medical notes for that day, Letby did not mention this incident with the mother. She claimed that it never happened and she was in another room at the time. The mother insists that it did happen and Letby was in that room with the infant. Was this Letby altering her medical notes to cover her tracks?

After the death of Child O, Letby wrote that peripheral access was lost on her clinical form. This was contradicted by other doctors who said this didn't happen. If Letby's notes had been accurate it would have been impossible for the baby to be injected with air. Coincidence? More track covering? The most famous article concerning doubts over Letby's conviction seems to be the one in the New Yorker. They failed to mention that Letby told the police she didn't really know what an air embolism was despite the fact she'd done a course on them in her nursing training. It failed to mention that Letby told the police she didn't know if she owned a paper shredder (to shred medical notes taken home) when in fact she had recently purchased one. There was no mention Dr Jayaram saying he walked on on her watching a baby crash. Letby is depicted in the New Yorker as being distraught and upset by baby deaths when in reality she was texting jokes, boasting about winning money on the Grand National, and always eager to go back to the special care unit as soon as possible. The New Yorker also failed to mention the close relationship (or alleged affair) she was having with a married doctor. There is even a theory that Letby was making babies collapse to get attention from this doctor.

The New Yorker didn't mention that Letby was using the medical handover sheets she'd taken home to gain access to online details about the families of the infants. The New Yorker made much of Dr Lee disputing the air embolism theory but when he was wheeled out for the appeal it turned out that he was not familiar with the multitude of other sources the prosecution had used and so turned out to be completely useless as a witness. It turned out the prosecution was not even using Dr Lee's diagnosis in the way he had assumed. The New Yorker suggested that it was difficult for the defence to get medical witnesses because they didn't want their image associated with a baby killing trial. The reality is that defence witnesses were hard to find because most experts thought Letby was guilty. Aside from Dr Hall, who was Ben Myers supposed to put in the witness box? Sarrita Adams? The police looked at half a million medical documents in their investigation. They split into teams so that their conclusions would be independent and not influenced by other investigations. Given the time and expense required for a criminal investigation, Cheshire Police were desperate for this to be a case of hospital negligence and for the deaths to be explainable. The last thing they wanted was a Beverly Allitt type case on their hands. No one involved in this case began with the desire to find a serial killer. That was the last thing any of them wanted.

The trial lasted ten months. Lucy Letby had one of the best barristers in the country at this trial. There was evidence from radiologists, blood experts, professors, neonatal experts, an endocrinologist, a forensic pathologist, doctors, consultants, nurses, parents. What more do you want? Maybe the biggest clue in this whole case was Letby in the witness box. Glum, defeated, disinterested, contradicting her police evidence at every turn, showing no emotion at the grim and tragic medical events being described in court. If none of these babies were the victim of foul play then that means all the medical professionals who gave evidence were wrong. It means the police were wrong. It means all the things that link Letby to this case were mere coincidences. While none of this is completely impossible it does seem rather a long shot doesn't it? The crux of the debate over Letby's guilt, if you attempt to boil it right down, as much as anything reduces to the fact that post-mortems were not immediately carried out again. Some experts say this makes it impossible to know for sure if Letby was guilty of what she was convicted of doing. Others would say there was more than sufficient evidence anyway. If she really is innocent you'd have to say that Letby must be one of the unluckiest nurses in the world to find herself at the scene of so many suspicious emergency situations.

THE CIRCLE

As you can see then, it is quite easy to write a chapter about all the reasons why Letby might be innocent and it is equally easy to write a chapter arguing that the conviction was sound. If you think Letby is innocent you can doubtless find holes in my chapter on why she is guilty and if you think she is guilty you can no doubt find holes in my chapter on why she is innocent. That's the way this game goes. Both sides can pick holes in one another's arguments and find details which favour their side of the fence. You have two possible scenarios here. The first scenario is that this was all a big mistake and an innocent woman is sitting in prison for horrendous fictional crimes she didn't commit. The second scenario is that a bunch of very misguided and mistaken people are basically cheerleading for a baby killer. We began this book by talking about miscarriages of justice. They do happen but they are not common. The justice system gets it right a lot more than they get it wrong. This fact though merely confirms the endless circle loop of arguments when it comes to Letby. Both sides can take something from this. Those who believe she is guilty can point out that most verdicts are sound. Those who believe she is innocent can point to the numerous cases where someone was convicted of awful crimes and later released when their innocence was proven.

As for how Letby might prove her innocence and avoid dying in prison, that is a question which is difficult to answer. In hindsight it was a mistake for Letby to give evidence at her trial and it was also a mistake not to allow Dr Hall (and other medical professionals) to be a defence witness. You had the combination of Letby's disastrous performance in the witness box and then the sight of Ben Myers KC trying to argue medical details with Dr Evans and others. Well briefed though he was, Ben Myers is not a doctor so this was never going to be ideal. The statistical evidence which Letby supporters make a fuss about probably wasn't very relevant either. Even if Ben Myers had put a statistician in the witness box, Letby would still be at HMP Bronzefield today because this was a case about medical evidence. Debating the methodology of the duty rota chart in the hospital might be a lot of fun for statisticians but isn't going to spring Lucy Letby from prison. To do that Letby's new barrister is probably going to have to come up with credible alternative explanations for what happened to the infants and this will require medical professionals of serious standing.

It won't be enough now to simply say the prosecution didn't prove their case. It is too late for that. Letby's legal representatives will have to come up with medical evidence which torpedoes the prosecution case. It won't be enough to say there was sewage or Letby did a lot of extra shifts. It won't be enough to say the insulin tests might have been wrong. Only time will tell if Letby is ever successful in quashing her convictions. It seems unlikely but stranger things have happened. A criticism of the Letby trial is that the jury had to follow and process complex medical information. Some feel it was unrealistic to expect members of the publicity to judge such a complicated case. But what is the alternative? A lot of cases are complex. Are we supposed to do anyway with having a jury and appoint a couple of experts to decide all criminal cases? The complaint that the jury was impartial or biased doesn't really hold water because they found Letby not guilty on some charges and were undecided on others.

The case of Lucy letby is very symbolic of the modern internet age where everyone with a keyboard is now the world's leading expert on everything. But most people are not experts in all the stuff they pontificate on in cyberspace. So you have the ridiculous spectacle of people sitting on their computer acting as if they know more about the medical evidence in this case than the doctors who worked at the hospital or spoke at the trial. A problem for the Letby supporters is that their movement, if we can call it that, was in part built on the back of Science on Trial. There is evidence that the New Yorker and the Guardian were very influenced by Sarrita Adams in their own pieces casting doubt on the case. This is an object lesson in making sure you have impeccable sources. Another problem with the more sympathetic Letby coverage is that they always seem to wheel out the same two or three statisticians for their quotes or 'evidence' that Letby could be innocent. What the Letby campaign (if that is the right term) really needs though is serious medical opinion - not statisticians.

Most of the people questioning the evidence online are plainly not qualified to second guess the doctors and experts who gave evidence at the trial. One must concede though that not everyone dubious about the Letby convictions falls into this category. Dr Svilena Dimitrova and Dr Michael Hall know their stuff and if they have doubts we should listen to them. It seems inevitable now that for as long as Letby is in prison you are going to have people insisting she is innocent. Even if she confessed to the crimes they'd probably ignore this and carry on campaigning as if nothing had happened. The endless circle of debate in the Letby case was encapsulated in the Thirwall Inquiry evidence where it was revealed that RPCPH reviewers in Chester did 'war games' on what might have happened to account for the spike in deaths and discussed air embolism, insulin poisoning and then two other possibilities which were redacted in the inquiry documents. The opposing camps in the Letby divide both took from this what they wanted to take. Those who believe she is guilty were inclined to feel this evidence proved that the doctors considered all possibilities and the inquiry was being open in acknowledging this. Those who believe Letby is innocent noted the redacted comments and largely saw them as evidence of a whitewash or cover-up.

Recent news has included a spike in neonatal deaths at a hospital in Shropshire which is not dissimilar to the spike in deaths at the hospital in Chester which triggered the Lucy Letby case. Reviews are now underway on the Shropshire hospital and the management have offered an apology for any sub-optimal care which may have occurred. It seems though (at the time of writing) that no serial killer theories have been floated and the police are not involved. The reviews and investigations strictly revolve around the standard of care and foul play doesn't seem to be something which has been seriously considered. Critics of the Letby convictions would understandably point to cases like this and argue this proves that spikes in infant deaths and sub-standard care in hospitals is sadly something which can and does happen. Letby supporters would probably argue that the Chester and Shropshire cases are quite similar - except for the fact that in the Shropshire case they didn't jump to illogical conclusions about a serial killer nurse. This is the foundation of the argument for those convinced Letby is innocent. They believe that natural causes and hospital shortcomings are much more plausible than the 'nice young nurse suddenly becomes serial killer' theory. They have a point too because on the face of it it does seem more plausible to pin the blame on sub-optimal care than a medical killer.

When you dig a little deeper though you can see the other

side of the coin. Dr Evans was not aware of Lucy Letby when he made his list of deaths which he deemed suspicious or hard to explain. Letby turned out to be on shift more than other nurses when it came to these incidents. At this point that isn't necessarily damning. We've established that Letby (who had a house to pay for) did a lot of extra shifts. But what Dr Evans didn't know was that Letby had all those handover medical notes and also did web searches on the families affected. He didn't know that Letby had written inaccurate medical notes for some of the infants in question. He didn't know that four consultants (the gang of four) had suspicions about Letby. He didn't know that Letby often seemed to offer her own counter diagnosis to colleagues in text messaging when it came to the infants. He didn't know that Letby seemed to be obsessed with working in the Nursery one unit with the more vulnerable babies and would often go in there even when she was supposed to be somewhere else.

If this was merely a case of a failing hospital and Letby was just an innocent oblivious nurse who found herself trapped in a Kafka-esque nightmare why was there all this weird circumstantial evidence linking her to the affected infants? And if this was strictly a case of bad care or infection how does one explain the insulin poisoning? Dr Dewi Evans, the main target for the Letby supporters, has, whether wisely or not, continued to speak to the media and even been willing to talk to critics through emails. He declared the Letby supporters 'poundshop Poirots' who have minimal information about the case and no access to the clinical records. Evans believes that because Letby was a white English nurse from a nice background that made it harder for people to accept her guilt. In an interview with The Sun, Dr Evans went through the key complaints that Letby supporters have about the case. On the issue of statistics, he said they were irrelevant and noted that the defence did not use a statistician at the trial.

On the issue of post-mortems not showing signs of foul play. Dr Evans said air embolisms don't show up on post-mortems and said the post-mortems were vital to the prosecution because they ruled out infection and haemorrhage. On the issue of Dr Shoo Lee, Evans pointed out that he used seventeen other sources for his air embolism theories and said his diagnosis of air embolism was not dependent on discovering this peculiar rash described by Dr Lee. Dr Evans also pointed out that other trial experts had backed his diagnosis despite being perfectly entitled to disagree or question them. Dr Evans said he was very satisfied with the insulin testing in the case and didn't understand how anyone could question the fact that insulin poisoning had taken place. On changing his mind about Child C (an air bubble was cited by the prosecution but it turned out Letby wasn't there at the time), Dr Evans said he was confident Letby used air to attack the child the next day and this explained why resuscitation failed. When it came to the popular theory that the hospital had a 'superbug', Dr Evans said that if the bacterium pseudomonas aeruginosa was in the bloodstream this would have been easily detected but it wasn't in the bloodstream and so wasn't detected.

"Over and above the troll stuff – ignore that – two groups of people have got themselves into a complete tizz about the case," Evans told the John Sweeney podcast. "First are the statisticians. The case had nothing to do with statistics. I'm not sure how many ways you can tell statisticians that the case had nothing to do with statistics. Secondly from neonatologists who had nothing to do with the case and should know better, who were not at the trial, did not see any of the clinical cases, did not read the statements from the local nurses and doctors, and are very unhappy that the trial went ahead. Time and time again the statisticians are just wrong. They are out of their depth. They do not understand what it is that leads to babies in the neonatal unit deteriorating, dying. Speaking to statisticians about this is a bit like speaking to a climate change denier or a Donald Trump supporter. It doesn't matter what you tell them, they don't want to know and that's that. They are welcome to their opinion. I spent 30 years on a neonatal unit, developing a neonatal intensive care service in Swansea. Your professor of statistics in London I'm sure is a very intelligent person, but I doubt whether he's spent 30 minutes in a neonatal unit unless one of his kids was a premature baby."

A big void in this case is the lack of a motive - though some have speculated that Letby suffered from Factitious disorder imposed on another. Factitious disorder imposed on another (aka Munchausen Syndrome by Proxy) is a mental health disorder in which a person intentionally produces, feigns, or exaggerates physical or psychological symptoms in another individual under their care. The individual may seek attention, validation, or a sense of control through the victim's illness. Some perpetrators may assume the role of a dedicated caregiver as a way to fulfil their own emotional needs. At the trial Nick Johnson KC said that Letby enjoyed 'playing God' with her patients. There is also the theory that Letby engineered these emergencies to get attention from 'Dr U' - who she was clearly very fond of. Not everyone is terribly convinced by this theory though and Letby denied that she 'loved' this doctor or was having an affair with him.

The woman at the heart of this debate remains something of a blank despite the fact that millions of words have been written about her. Who is the real Lucy Letby? Serial killer or victim of injustice? We know that Letby had a comfortable (if not wealthy) background and came from a loving family.

There is nothing dark or sinister about her past. Her life was alarmingly normal. She went to work. Had drinks with friends. Watched television. Most of the hospital staff who gave evidence seemed to be quite fond of Letby. Most of them said she was a good nurse. Letby seems to be a Zelig like character in reports from colleagues and court correspondents. Some depict her as shy and quiet while others say she is confident and pushy. In court she was described as mumbling and scared by some but as crisp and confident by others. One feature of the court reports is that Letby refused to make eye contact with the prosecution barrister Nick Johnson. There are all manner of possible interpretations as to why she would do this.

The fact that Letby seemed mundane and normal in real life is not unheard of when it comes to serial killers. Harold Shipman was an unassuming chap who liked to cultivate vegetables in his garden. No one who knew Shipman had him pegged as a serial killer. Serial killers come in all shapes and sizes. They aren't always easy to spot. Ted Bundy looked like a politician or a game show host. "The night that we arrested Fred West," said Tony Butler, the chief constable of Gloucestershire Police at the time, "the TV crews were in Cromwell Street and I remember on the Points West news, neighbours saying: No no, the police have got this all wrong. Fred and Rose, lovely family couple, lovely family people. And they clearly weren't." Rose West was certainly an unlikely looking sadistic sexually motivated serial killer by the time she was arrested. She resembled a frumpy old granny. Even so, it is difficult to square the smiling pictures of Lucy Letby in her blue nurses uniform with the things she was convicted of doing. If she is guilty then Letby must be a deeply disturbed person. A real Jekyll & Hyde.

This is surely at least one component of why so many people

refuse to believe she is guilty. It is not the most important component but Letby's mundane and benign appearance hardly screams serial killer. Lucy Letby looked like someone on the cover of an NHS brochure. She was the visual epitome of the heroes we were told to outside and give a round of applause to during covid. Even her name is strangely appealing. Lucy Letby. LL. If a short man with a giant beard and coke bottle spectacles named Len Trubshaw had been convicted of these crimes would the internet have been so exercised in a campaign on his behalf? The case of Victorino Chua (the male nurse convicted of killing patients at Stepping Hill Hospital) is quite similar to that of Letby in a number of ways but aside from a ghost town Facebook group one will find scant online evidence of people campaigning or advocating for Chua. Is this because Chua is a portly middle-aged man from the Philippines? Critics of Letby's conviction would probably argue that her prosecution is less watertight than that of Chua but you get my point.

Letby might not be the most obvious serial killer in the world (and by that I suppose I'm saying that she didn't look mad or crazy) but she did fit a pattern in that the overwhelming majority of female killers work in the health system and don't use guns or knives. Female killers are more likely to use poison than their male counterparts and are generally regarded to be less gruesome. 'They're often described as quiet killers,' wrote Discover Magazine of female serial killers. 'They typically don't butcher, nor torture. They prefer poison — in 50 percent of all cases — and smothering to conspicuous knives and guns. They also tend to kill at home or at work, drawing less attention than the random, far-flung sprees common among men. In a 2013 paper analysing the characteristics of female serial killers, sociologist Amanda Farrell wrote that they kill, on average, over longer stretches of time than their male counterparts.'

So you've now, the undecided agnostics aside, got two camps who both have their own completely different version of Lucy Letby. To those who are certain she is guilty she is an evil and manipulative serial killer with a charge sheet that places her on an infamous pedestal with the likes of Bevery Allitt. To those who are certain she is innocent she is a caring and lovely woman who has been victimised by a corrupt and incompetent health system and judiciary. They can perhaps imagine a day when Letby walks free from prison into the arms of her campaigners and supporters as champagne corks fly. She'll go straight to the This Morning studios for an interview and be greeted as a victim and hero. A brave survivor of injustice. It's like a true crime online culture war. But does it matter? In the long run it probably doesn't.

Someone with 164 Twitter followers posting endlessly that Dr Evans is an idiot or Dr Jaryam is a liar is not going to quash the convictions. No amount of reposted photographs of Lucy Letby in nurse uniform and Christmas antlers will cut any ice with the Court of Appeal. Amateur medical experts on forums furiously seeking to discredit or invalidate the evidence of prosecution witnesses at the trial and inquiry are wasting their time. Online petitions won't change anything either. The only thing that will ever get Letby out of prison is her barrister finding enough expert medical opinion to cast serious doubt on the prosecution. That will be a very tall order. One camp believes the conviction against Letby is sound and she will spend the rest of her life in prison. The other camp seem to believe that one day this whole case will fall apart and Letby will be released. They can't both be right though can they? Only time will tell if the strange case of Lucy Letby has a big twist up its sleeve.

SOURCES

https://thirlwall.public-inquiry.uk/
https://nation.cymru/news
https://www.bmj.com/content/386/bmj.q1487/rapid-responses
https://www.theguardian.com
https://www.telegraph.co.uk
https://www.wimbledonguardian.co.uk
https://www.bbc.co.uk
https://www.labpulse.com
https://www.judiciary.uk/
https://assets.caselaw.nationalarchives.gov.uk/ewca/crim/2024/748/ewca_crim_2024_748.pdf
/news/national/24654026.cold-letby-initially-failed-final-year-student-nurse-placement-probe-told/
https://www.chesterstandard.co.uk/

Photo Credit

Unknown

19th august 2023

https://www.bbc.co.uk/news/uk-66104004